Shine On!

# SHINE

## Five Principles for a Rewarding Life

Kris Den Besten

DESTINY IMAGE® PUBLISHERS, INC.
P.O. Box 310, Shippensburg, PA 17257-0310

***"Speaking to the Purposes of God for this Generation and for the Generations to Come."***

This book and all other Destiny Image, Revival Press, Mercy Place, Fresh Bread, Destiny Image Fiction, and Treasure House books are available at Christian bookstores and distributors worldwide.

For a U.S. bookstore nearest you, call 1-800-722-6774.

For more information on foreign distributors, call 717-532-3040.

Or reach us on the Internet: www.destinyimage.com.

ISBN 10: 0-7684-2608-1
ISBN 13: 978-0-7684-2608-3

For Worldwide Distribution, Printed in the U.S.A.

1 2 3 4 5 6 7 8 9 10 11 / 09 08

# Endorsements

Kris Den Besten lives a life of mission, purpose, vision, and values. In this book, Kris reveals the powerful vision that helped him to transform his work and life. I encourage you to read and reflect on the principles he shares in this book and, most importantly, to commit to living by its light. Be prepared to SHINE!

John C. Maxwell
Founder of INJOY Stewardship Services and EQUIP
Motivational Speaker
Author of numerous books including
*Thinking for a Change, Developing the Leader Within You, Ethics 101, Talent is Never Enough,* and *Life@Work*

In the workplace today, many people are looking for more significance in their work. Many have questions about how to integrate their faith into their work. This book gives inspirational guidance on how to integrate faith and work on a daily basis. It also challenges readers to find true significance and servanthood in their daily life and work.

Mary Vermeer Andringa
President/CEO, Vermeer Corporation
www.vermeer.com

At Interstate Batteries, values and principles play a critical role in directing all of our business decisions. In *SHINE,* Kris Den Besten reveals a powerful message about how godly values can significantly impact not only our work but also our lives and the lives of others. I recommend this book to anyone who wants their work to truly matter . . . forever.

Norm Miller
Chairman, Interstate Batteries

Kris has written a powerful volume that will both inform and inspire all who desire to effectively exalt Christ in the marketplace. Kris is a leader of character and competence, integrity and influence. He is uniquely qualified to write this book. You must read it.

Doug Carter
Senior Vice President, EQUIP, a ministry of John C. Maxwell

Kris Den Besten's genuine commitment to the SHINE principles advanced in this eminently practical book is evidenced not only in his writing, but in his day-to-day business practices. As a wife, and mother of two of his employees, I am grateful for the way Den Besten leads his company and cares for those under his employ. As a business professional I value the wise, pragmatic counsel this book offers. I recommend you read this insightful book and then share it with your family and co-workers.

MARILYN JEFFCOAT
President, Total Sculpt

This book should be a helpful tool for anyone who is a committed follower of Jesus Christ and desires to integrate the claims of their faith with the demands of their work.

BILL POLLARD
Chairman Emeritus, ServiceMaster
Author, *Soul of the Firm* and *Serving Two Masters*

# Contents

INTRODUCTION

# The SHINE Vision

I used to go to work to earn a living. Like many others, my work was all about surviving, paying bills, and getting by. Over time, the allure of success altered my work into an obsession that ran my life. A yearning to reach beyond success and climb toward significance eventually set in. Regrettably, the more personal success I tasted, the seemingly less significant my life at work became. I began to doubt that my career held any true lasting value.

Fortunately, that began to change a few years ago as our employees and I embraced a new vision for doing business. This vision first began taking shape and transforming my life at work. It then began to positively influence all other aspects of my daily walk.

During the process, our company experienced impressive growth and increased profitability. In addition, job satisfaction soared as many of us began to experience a much greater sense of reward and fulfillment from our labors.

It's true that I still earn a living when I go to work. However, through the power of this illuminating vision, I am now convinced that my work life—and yours—has the potential to rise above survival, to soar past success, and to shine beyond significance.

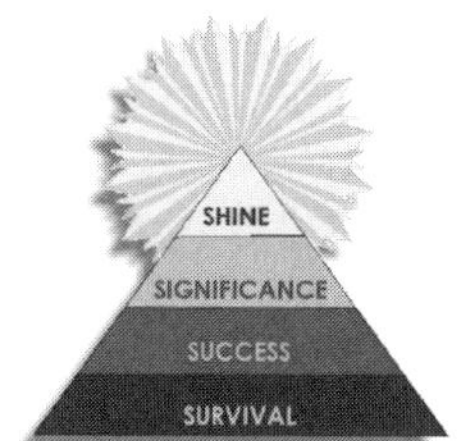


THE SHINE VISION

***Living by vision is to be motivated by what could be, rather than being held back by what is.***

## CATCH THE SHINE VISION

It was clearly a defining moment. The leader called his key team members together for a corporate retreat. Each individual sensed the excitement of what was coming. Perched upon a breathtaking vista overlooking a shimmering body of water, he explained a new vision to inspire the team. This new vision would set them apart while providing the ultimate competitive advantage. Where many had established ritual, rules, and strict processes for conducting business, this leader implored his people to search deeply inside themselves. His vision called for a radical departure from the status quo—in order to embrace a revolutionary perspective. Instead of focusing on proper procedure, this vision focused on becoming and being people of character.

With unforeseen authority, the leader eloquently wove together the elements of mission, purpose, vision, values, and relationships. His words motivated and lifted the countenance of each individual. This vision required far beyond mere compliance to standards. Rather, it called for complete commitment of each individual's heart, soul, mind, and strength. All previous management models had to be discarded for the new way.

This way would not be easy. But for those who chose to embody the vision, the ultimate benefit would stretch beyond hope or imagination. This vision would prove so compelling that, once embraced, it would shine from generation to generation.

Many things have changed since Jesus first cast this vision nearly two thousand years ago on a hillside overlooking the Sea of Galilee. Yet one thing remains vividly clear: the source of light for this vision is the same yesterday, today, and tomorrow. The vision is simple. We are called to SHINE—to live in such a way that others would see Christ's character radiating in us to the glory of God the Father.

> *Let your light so shine before men, that they may see your good works and glorify your Father in Heaven* (Matt. 5:16 NKJV).

Admittedly, it took me a while to realize to whom Jesus was speaking when He cast that vision to shine. Clearly, this vision could not apply to me. I reasoned it was just intended for the disciples who joined Him on the mount that day, or for pastors and missionaries—surely not for tractor salesmen. My work was built around selling equipment, growing a business, and seeking greater future success. Consequently, there was not much happening in my work day that glorified my Father in Heaven.

## RISE ABOVE SURVIVAL

Located in central Iowa, Vermeer Manufacturing Company builds construction equipment. In 1967, two of its young employees left Iowa and moved across the country to start a new dealership called Vermeer Southeast. My father established the company's headquarters in Florida, and his partner ran the first branch office in Georgia.

By the late 1980s, the business was grossing around $4 million a year. About that time, I joined the company as a raw trainee. Over the next few years, my career blossomed as our revenues grew substantially, and I eventually became the CEO and majority shareholder of our company.

During that period, my success as a businessman was invigorating and impressive. Yet, even as I pushed our company to grow the bottom line, to break more sales records, and to make more money, I began to feel less and less fulfilled in my work. A sense that I was missing something began to set in. But I wasn't sure what that was.

While all of this was happening in business, I continued to attend church services most Sundays. However, I was not connected. I made time for Sunday worship, but that was it. The responsibilities of running a business and chasing success kept me too preoccupied to do any more. The trap had been set—juggling God-worship on Sunday morning and self-worship the rest of the week—and I was caught. My work had become my god.

## SOAR PAST SUCCESS

That's when I began to realize my work life needed a change. I was sharing with a mentor my guilty feelings of not doing more significant things—like church work. Her response was enlightening: "Maybe God wants to use you where you have the most influence. Right now that might not be in your church. Perhaps God wants to use you in a significant way for His glory in the business He's given you."

That statement hit me hard. It was difficult to fathom glorifying God while working in tractor sales. Then a new light inside of me began to come on. God began to clearly reveal my own vision for my life and work, which is based on Matthew 5:16: to shine with excellence. The core of this vision is that God is glorified when His character is revealed through us. From that perspective, our work can become our real life ministry. Regardless of position or profession, anyone can shine when Christ is seen in them.

In 2001, we were coming off of another record year in total revenues. Much of that came from selling construction equipment used to build the fiber optic infrastructure for the Internet. That same year, most of this major construction came to a sudden halt. Then the stock market went into freefall. A few months later, the terrorist attack of 9-11 gave our business what could have been its final blow. By the end of the year, we had lost more than half of our revenues compared to the prior year.

Despite this bleak financial picture, our company was about to embark on something much more valuable than any financial asset. We desperately needed to transport our values and mission statement from the walls of our buildings and into the hearts of our people. This new vision—to shine with excellence—would prove essential for guidance in such trying times.

## SHINE BEYOND SIGNIFICANCE

The economical collapse of 2001 affected a lot of people in our industry. Many equipment dealerships went out of business. Some of our biggest customers filed for bankruptcy. Employee layoffs and facility shutdowns became common.

Eventually, as this tough year approached its close, it came time for our annual Christmas party. In previous years, this social occasion had provided an opportunity to celebrate our success as a company, pat ourselves on the back for our outstanding numbers, and then pass out bonus checks to everyone. In the light of the down-turn of the past year, what would we do at this corporate gathering? The mood going into the party was certainly not celebratory. Our employees knew what was going on. Some worried about their jobs. Some even questioned if we, as a company, could survive.

On the way to the dinner, I discussed with my wife the desire to shift our company focus away from the numbers and toward a new scoreboard. We needed a new standard by which to measure ourselves—something based on living out our values and pursuing this new vision to shine with excellence. "Maybe you could sum all that up with the word *SHINE*," she said. "Then your vision could become more clearly defined."

I looked over our mission/values statement again and the SHINE acronym immediately came to mind. This acronym outlines the five principles that are the foundation of the SHINE vision:

**S**–Serve Others (Principle #1)
**H**–Honor God (Principle #2)
**I**–Improve Continually (Principle #3)
**N**–Navigate by Values (Principle #4)
**E**–Excel in Relationships (Principle #5)

That night I introduced our employees to this new scoreboard. We would still monitor the numbers. We, however, now would measure ourselves by how well we lived out our vision to shine. I believed that if we would focus on these key principles, everything else would take care of itself. I explained to the employees that living by vision is to be motivated by what could be, rather than being held back by what is.

The staff clapped politely. However, it was not until we handed out bonus checks—even though we had lost money that year—that the concept took hold. It was then that they began to catch the vision. It is true that people believe what they see much more than what they hear. And those bonus checks spoke more powerfully than anything I could have said. In the same way our witness for Christ is most impacting when He is seen in our actions rather than just proclaimed by our words.

Financially, the year that followed was not much better. Even so, we made a small profit without laying off a single employee or closing a single store. Since 2001, the SHINE vision has been the beacon which guides our company. Our fiscal results speak for themselves as annual sales have grown to nearly $100 million. We have expanded our business through acquisitions and new store start-ups. Our company has never been stronger, financially or structurally.

But the SHINE vision is about more than just improving numbers and expanding our business. It is about a radical shift in setting our priorities and gauging our success. With this new kind of scoreboard, we see things in a new light.. Like all companies, we still face challenges and sometimes fall short of goals. The SHINE vision, however, helps keep us on track and propels us toward opportunities, as an organization and as individuals, to shine.

## IGNITE THE SHINE VISION

The SHINE vision is based on three key exhortations given by Jesus to honor God, advance His Kingdom, and reflect His glory:

### 1. The Great Commandment: Honor God

> *You shall love the Lord your God with all your heart, with all your soul, with all your mind, and with all your strength . . .* (Mark 12:30 NKJV).

### 2. The Great Commission: Advance God's Kingdom

> *All authority has been given to Me in Heaven and on earth. Go therefore and make disciples of all the nations, baptizing them in the name of the Father and of the Son and of the Holy Spirit, teaching them to observe all things I have commanded you . . .* (Matt. 28:18-20 NKJV).

### 3. The Great Empowerment: Reflect God's Glory

> *. . . And lo, I am with you always, even to the end of the age* (Matt. 28:20 NKJV).

> *Let your light so shine before men, that they may see your good works and glorify your Father in Heaven* (Matt. 5:16 NKJV).

The SHINE vision is not some kind of how-to formula to make you employee of the month or salesperson of the quarter—although that could very well happen. Rather, it is a biblically-based, Christ-centered approach for transforming the objective of our work from making a living to making a difference. I am convinced that embracing and applying the five SHINE principles will strengthen your character, improve your career, and lead you to greater fulfillment in all aspects of life. Most importantly, you will be building a legacy of Christ's work in and through you to impact the world around you. As you read this book, please note that SHINE is not something we can do on our own. We cannot shine for God in and of ourselves. Only He can shine in us.

## Principle One

# SERVE OTHERS

*For even the Son of Man came not to be served but to serve others and to give His life as a ransom for many* (Matthew 20:28 NLT).

# Chapter 1

# Ignite the Flame of Servanthood

### A HEART OF SERVANTHOOD GLORIFIES GOD BY HELPING OTHERS

*. . . But the greatest among you shall be your servant* (Matthew 23:11).

Max DePree, former CEO of a global leader in office furnishings, once said, "The first responsibility of a leader is to define reality. The last is to say thank you. In between the two, the leader must become a servant and a debtor."[1] Learning this concept has proven a powerful lesson for me. During the 1990s, our company experienced exponential growth, an accomplishment for which I took much of the credit. During those high-growth years, I climbed from salesman to sales manager to general manager and eventually to owner.

My success came with an unhealthy dose of pride. As the son of the company founder, I felt the added pressure to prove myself to those around me, including my dad. One day, soon after I had been appointed sales manager, I closed the biggest deal in the history of our company. It was a multi-million-dollar deal to a customer who, up to that point, had bought almost exclusively from our competitor. Upon finalizing the order, I waltzed into my dad's office, filled with self-delight, and proclaimed, "I got the deal!"

He reached out to congratulate me. Instead of saying thank you, I grabbed his hand and said, "What's the biggest deal you ever closed, Dad?"

My father sat down in his chair and frowned. I knew he could not come up with a deal to top mine because there had never been one. Eventually his answer came, but it was not what I expected. "You know," he said, as he gave me one of those looks only a father can give his son, "I can't say that any particular transaction stands out in my mind. But I guess I take the most pride in knowing that this company has provided for so many families for so many years, and that God has allowed me to be part of it."

How could I respond to that? I made no comment as I, ashamedly enlightened about my own arrogance, slithered back to my office. My dad had clearly defined leadership for me. My focus had been on applauding myself in the mirror when it should have been on looking out the window, encouraging others and praising God.

At that point, I began to comprehend the responsibility of serving our people. Success had been all about me; significance would be all about them. For the first time, the correlation between greatness and serving began to resonate within me. True significance is never found in serving self, but only in serving others.

## SERVE PASSIONATELY

***Service.*** The meaning of this word has various connotations. We use it to identify those who serve on committees, wait on tables, or fix things when they break. Service may be defined as work done as a job, duty, punishment, or favor for somebody else. Typically, the word *service* implies an action, usually temporary, that is done in a sense of obligation and carries limited reward for the server.

This is a common perspective in the workplace where we serve our time earning a wage. But why is this? The typical workplace commonly fosters a "me first" environment. In that setting, work can become a place of exhaustive self-service, of climbing the corporate ladder, and of looking out for number one. We serve to get ahead, to make more money, to be credited for our contributions. Work becomes all about us and what we want. When our service is all about us, we labor to make a living. Self-focused service performed out of obligation can leave us—like slaves to our work—empty and downtrodden. However, we can change that.

**Servanthood suggests that we put the needs of others before our own, regardless of circumstances.** Our service is not controlled by our environment. Rather, it is a choice made in the heart. God places us in the workplace to serve others. He calls us to genuinely care about the needs, the dreams, the hopes, and the hurts of those around us. He wants us to see others as He sees them: people in need.

**Servanthood has as its mission to glorify God by helping others.** Our service, then, is no longer viewed as duty or an obligation. Rather, it is an opportunity to do the good works God has planned for us. Our ultimate service is to God, who uses us to do good works which glorify Him. This provides us with a fresh way of looking at our work.

**Servanthood stimulates our hearts while it adjusts our focus.** A heart of servanthood is clearly committed to caring for the welfare and serving for the benefit of others. Through fostering a heart of servanthood, we begin to understand that our acts of service become a blessing that we pass on to others. We no longer serve out of obligation, but we serve out of love as we reflect the heart of Christ to those we encounter. "If anyone serves, he should do it with the strength God provides, so that in all things God may be praised through Jesus Christ . . . " (1 Peter 4:11b).

## SERVE PROFESSIONALLY

Our work provides countless opportunities to serve needs and to reveal the heart of servanthood. Business essentially is all about serving others. For a business to survive it must consistently accomplish two things:

1. Serve a need.
2. Make a profit.

It is important to note the order of these two critical elements. For a business to exist, it must first serve a need. For continued existence it must then make a profit. For enduring success, a business must continue to do both.

**Servanthood requires the proper order of priorities: people before profit.** I have heard it said that profit is a lot like oxygen. You need it to survive. However, oxygen is not life itself. Likewise, contrary to popular belief, profit is not what business is all about. A company that shines realizes that serving others is the life of the company and that profit, like oxygen, sustains the company and allows it to continue serving.

We need to serve the needs of employees and fellow workers. Individuals give their best effort in an environment where they are served, appreciated, and cared for. When we put our employees first and serve them with sincerity, they generally respond with inner motivation, which insures the company's profit.

---

**Most businesses serve for profit rather than profiting from serving.**

---

We need to serve the needs of customers. In business, the concept of serving customers is of great importance. Most companies realize that if they serve the customer, then they'll get more business. Consequently, most businesses serve for profit rather than profiting from serving. They serve the customer strictly to sell more stuff.

Servanthood requires more than that. True servants are motivated wholly by helping others. They don't serve for what it could do for them but for what it will do for those they serve. Servants choose to focus on how they can positively impact their organization by helping others meet challenges and improve their professional and personal lives.

Professional servants put no limits on whom they will serve. A servant-hearted professional willingly serves customers, subordinates, leaders, fellow associates, suppliers, and anyone else with whom they come into contact.

## SERVE UNSELFISHLY

Unfortunately, the workplace is flooded with those whose sole intent lies in serving themselves. Consequently, the concept of servanthood seems almost foreign in today's business world. Can you imagine a company where the CEO or owner would believe that their greatest responsibility was not to the bottom line but to serving the employees of the company? What if employees, instead of focusing on their own personal needs and desires, began to look first at serving others? What if we all stopped focusing on how valuable we think we are to the cause and in turn started focusing on bringing the most value to everyone we encounter at work? Think of the difference that could make.

Scripture provides us with the great paradox of serving: " . . . Whoever wants to become great among you must be your servant, and whoever wants to be first must be your slave" (Matt. 20:26-27). Jesus made it very clear that the way to greatness in God's Kingdom is not found in serving ourselves but in serving others. This servanthood concept is not just suggested for future reward, but it is to be whole heartedly embraced and exemplified right now as our service represents His kingdom on earth.

God sees and records all of our acts of service. He knows and understands the motives of our hearts. He promises to exalt those who reveal the true heart of servanthood. In essence, the most effective way to serve ourselves is by unselfishly serving others. The more we serve, the more valuable we become to others and the more we increase our own value. Interestingly, truly selfless service tends to return truly significant rewards. Albert Schweitzer said, "I don't know what your destiny will be. But one thing I know: The only ones among you who will be really happy are those who have sought and found how to serve."

## SERVE FAITHFULLY

God has equipped each of us to serve. By serving others, we simultaneously serve Him. One of the easiest ways to prepare our hearts for serving others is through prayer. Praying for others inexplicably transports their needs directly to the heart level. If you find yourself dealing with a difficult customer or colleague, try praying for them by name. Ask God to use your interaction with them as a blessing to their life. It's amazing how much easier it is to serve someone for whom you're praying. As an employee, what greater display of servanthood could you show your employer than to pray for the company, its leaders, and your fellow employees?

If you are in leadership, how often do you lift the names of those you lead in prayer? My company has over 200 employees spread over fifteen locations. Although I don't have a close personal relationship with every employee, I can still pray for them by name. An interesting thing happens when I lift each employee's name in prayer. My depth of caring grows as I pray for each of them. Prayer is such a simple act of service, yet so often a forgotten one, especially in the workplace.

---

**A heart of servanthood glorifies God by helping others.**

---

To understand service that shines, we need only look at the example of Jesus, who willingly stepped down from His heavenly throne, taking the role of a servant on earth (see Phil. 2:5-9). Through His readiness to serve the needs of others, Jesus revealed the true heart of God in servanthood. In order to serve others like Christ, we too must be willing to reveal the heart of servanthood. It is only through the purity of a servant's heart that Christ's light can shine in us. Inside each of us is a heart equipped for serving others—we just need to let it show.

A servant heart radiates *humility* to reach beyond ourselves, *compassion* to care for others, and *generosity* to help others find success. We, therefore, simply should do as Scripture directs: "Each one should use whatever gift he has received to serve others, faithfully administering God's grace in its various forms" (1 Peter 4:10).

---

**Endnote**

1. Max DePree, *Leadership Is an Art* (New York: Dell Publishing, 1989), 11.

## Chapter 2

# Shine With Humility

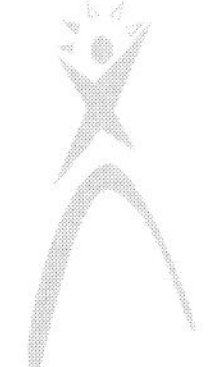

### PUT OTHERS FIRST

*Do nothing out of selfish ambition or vain conceit, but in humility consider others better than yourselves* (Philippians 2:3).

A few years ago, I stopped at a job site to check on some of our guys. They were demonstrating a machine to a potential buyer, and I wanted to help. Our guys were using an underground boring machine to install a new fiber optic line under the parking lot of a business complex. They had run into a problem. An old piece of plastic pipe had wrapped itself around the rods of our tunneling machine, stopping it cold.

We all knew what had to be done. Someone had to crawl into a mud hole and cut away the pipe. Since our team had been working hard all day, I volunteered. Quickly, I changed into a pair of shorts and climbed down into the mud, which instantly engulfed me from head to toe. Hooting and hollering, the guys took great advantage of the situation. I, of course, played along. Thirty minutes later, however, when I climbed out of the hole with the mission accomplished, everyone cheered.

Wearing only my filthy shorts and a good ten pounds of mud, I was feeling pretty good as I waddled toward my truck. About that time, the owner of the company for which we were demonstrating the machine pulled up. Not even getting out of his vehicle, he took one look at me, rolled down the window, and asked me where my boss was. Without speaking, I shrugged and motioned my hands as if to say, "You're looking at him."

His face grew flushed as he began to scream, "You are totally unprofessional and unsafe! How can you show up on a jobsite looking like that? Get off my job right now!"

At that point, I just got into my truck and drove away. To this day, I don't know if he ever realized that I actually was the boss. What really mattered is that we finished the job and sold the machine. Swallowing your pride can be quite humbling, which I can attest to. Ultimately, however, it can prove very rewarding.

## LET GO OF EGO

Humility is putting others first. However, it is tough to be humble when our own egos keep getting in the way. Ego-related problems make it hard to be humble:

- **Inflated ego.** Too much pride leads to selfish ambition and fosters an unhealthy ego. Pride makes it difficult to put the needs of others before our own.
- **Deflated ego.** Too little pride limits a sense of self worth and causes an individual to question how they could possibly benefit someone else.
- **Fragile ego.** Some try to mask their own insecurities by projecting a false sense of over–confidence, resulting in an air of arrogance.

The typical work place overflows with ego issues. Fortunately, humility can soothe every type of ego problem. Humility places our focus onto others and allows our egos to slip into the background. Regardless of the state of our egos, Scripture points to humility as the catalyst for long-term, significant advancement: " . . . All of you clothe yourselves with humility toward one another, because 'God opposes the proud but gives grace to the humble.' Humble yourselves, therefore, under God's mighty hand, that he may lift you up in due time" (1 Pet. 5:5-6).

*Good to Great,* the best-selling book by Jim Collins, examines good companies which, over time, became really great companies. Collins' research reveals a fascinating fact. In all the top-performing companies, the good-to-great transitions came under the leadership of what he calls a Level 5 leader. Collins explains, "Level 5 leaders channel their ego needs away from themselves and into the larger goal of building a great company."[1]

---

**HUMILITY ALLOWS US TO BE THE TYPE OF LEADER GOD CALLS US TO BE.**

---

It was not the charismatic, self-promoting, bigger-than-life CEOs who led these top companies. It was humble servants who were willing to lay aside their egos to serve the needs of the organization. Level 5 leaders are defined by Collins as having a great mix of personal humility and professional will. They approach their work not so much for what it will get them but more for how they can contribute to the overall cause.

> *Be shepherds of God's flock that is under your care, serving as overseers—not because you must, but because you are willing, as God wants you to be; not greedy for money, but eager to serve; not lording it over those entrusted to you, but being examples to the flock* (1 Peter 5:2-3).

## LET GO OF ENTITLEMENT

Face it: We all like to be served. Most of us crave the feeling of self-importance and take great pleasure when others serve our needs. Perhaps, in holding a title or a position at work that requires others to serve us, we begin to feel entitled to it. How easy it is to slip into the entitlement mindset. We believe we have earned the right to be served. Unfortunately, the tighter we cling to our rights, the further we repel from possessing a humble heart.

If we have been burned by someone in the past and are feeling entitled to seeking vengeance, humility allows us to let go and to not seek to even the score. Scripture calls for us to forgive those who trespass against us, no matter how difficult that may be (see Matt. 18:21-35).

Throughout the years, we have uncovered a few instances of employees stealing, in one way or another, from our company. Just the thought of a team member stealing from our organization used to fill me with rage. Over time, I have come to realize our responsibility to enforce the consequences for the behavior and, also, to forgive the person and not hold a grudge. Each of these breaches of trust has led to termination of the employee from our company—and to forgiveness for the individual. The consequence of termination frees our company of unacceptable behavior, while at the same time, forgiveness frees our hearts from the perceived right for reprisal. A humble heart is free from resentment and grudges.

> *Get rid of all bitterness, rage, anger, harsh words, and slander, as well as all types of evil behavior. Instead, be kind to each other, tenderhearted, forgiving one another, just as God through Christ has forgiven you* (Ephesians 4:31-32 NLT).

Forgiveness, at times, may seem completely impractical. Yet we are called to forgive others as Christ has forgiven us. This requires the humility to continually ask ourselves:

- Are there perceived rights of which I need to let go?
- Do I need to seek forgiveness from someone?
- Is there someone I need to forgive?

Forgiveness is at the core of a humble heart. Whether granting or receiving it, forgiveness is a freeing experience that opens our hearts to experience joy.

## PICK UP JOY

Humility is a tough quality to live out. It demands that we relinquish our rights in order to take on responsibilities. When we relinquish our right to be served and willingly take on the responsibility of serving others, we open ourselves to a much more joyful and fulfilling work life.

As the CEO of our company, I carry a lot of pressure to get things done. Occasionally someone will drop the ball, drag things out, or just not comprehend what we are trying to accomplish. In these instances, it is my responsibility to hold others accountable, clearly communicate expectations, and keep the company moving ahead together. My natural tendency, however, is to make a quick decision and plow ahead regardless of other viewpoints. I reason, "I'm the CEO and they work for me. They'll do what I say." True, this keeps us moving. However, that attitude is not a proper reflection of our Lord. I know that we are to reflect God's glory in all we do. Still, at times, I have to catch myself to keep from reacting in a thoughtless self-centered manner. Consequently, there is a familiar, simple acronym I like to use to remind me of how I should react when the grip on my rights gets so tight I can't let go:

**J** — Jesus
**O** — Others
**Y** — Yourself

If we view our work from this perspective, the grip on rights weakens and allows humility to shine through us. By focusing on Jesus first, we concurrently serve others. It does not soften our responsibility in any way. It just leads us forward in a much more cohesive fashion. If we approach our duties with this joy, we are much more likely to gain buy-in and support from others. Our strength to accomplish this comes directly from God:

> *The Lord is my strength and shield. I trust Him with all my heart. He helps me, and my heart is filled with joy . . .* (Psalm 28:7 NLT).

Serving others brings far more joy than does serving ourselves. That is why the roots for a life of joy grow deepest in the soil of humility.

## PICK UP STRENGTH

Often the word *humility* is misconstrued as weakness, when true humility actually provides great strength. It takes more than our own strength to overcome selfish desires and to put others first. If someone is rude or arrogant toward us, humility provides the strength to remain upbeat and secure, despite their words or behavior. In fact, Christ-like humility opens our hearts to receive supernatural strength. Through humility, we tap into the power of God and don't have to worry about what others may think or say about us. We are secure and strong enough in Him to serve confidently, regardless of the situation.

Jesus displayed a perfect example of the strength found in humility. Notice the position of strength from which Jesus came as He humbly served His followers:

> *Jesus knew that the Father had put all things under His power, and that He had come from God and was returning to God; so He got up from the meal . . . poured water into a basin and began to wash His disciples' feet, drying them with the towel that was wrapped around Him* (John 13:3-5).

It was with great strength and authority that Jesus lovingly relinquished the right to be served and, instead, chose to serve with humility.

Through salvation in Jesus Christ, we are the children of God and, therefore, His representatives on earth right now, in all we do. It is from this position of our inherited Kingdom authority that we are empowered to serve others with the strength of humility.

## PUT OTHERS FIRST

A few years ago, the leaders of our company met to define our key operational objectives. Up to that point, our goals and objectives had always focused on selling more equipment and products while increasing our revenues. It was time to redirect our focus from selling machinery to serving people. We adopted the following objectives, which better define our corporate priorities of who—and how—we serve:

**Objective 1: Honor God**

We will honor God as faithful stewards of resources and relationships.

**Objective 2: Promote Teamwork**

We will accomplish our vision together by uniting skills and efforts around common goals.

**Objective 3: Employee Growth**

We will help our employees reach their full potential by developing their skills and promoting their well-being.

**Objective 4: Customer Satisfaction**

We will provide service and support to build loyal relationships and earn recommendations.

**Objective 5: Profit Growth**

We will use profits to grow and improve, to provide for needs, and to affect our community in positive ways.

---

**SERVE OTHERS THROUGH HUMILITY—PUT OTHERS FIRST.**

---

We have found that seeking these objectives keeps us humble and takes the focus off of individual agendas. First and foremost, we as a company desire to serve God with humility. We don't preach or try to force our beliefs on anyone. Yet, we make it clear what we believe and who we ultimately desire to serve. Not every employee is a Christian. It's certainly not a requirement of employment to work at our company.

However, our corporate focus on serving God brings a confident sense of security to each employee, regardless of their system of beliefs.

Teamwork develops humility by promoting the well-being of our team over any individual while seeking a common mission. Serving our employees by training, encouraging, and empowering them equips everyone for better service. Finally, a humble focus on people before profit, relationships before revenues, and others before self leads to continual growth, positive impact, and greater opportunities. A humble workplace can indeed be a rewarding workplace.

---

### Endnote

1. Jim Collins, *Good to Great* (New York: Harper Collins, 2001), 22.

# Chapter 3

# Shine With Compassion

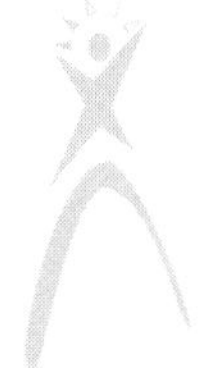

## SHOW YOU CARE

*But when He saw the multitudes, He was moved with compassion for them, because they were weary and scattered, like sheep having no shepherd*
(Matthew 9:36 NKJV).

The devastation Hurricane Katrina dealt to the coastal areas of Mississippi and Louisiana was shocking. A friend of mine relayed his first-hand experience of participating in a New Orleans rescue mission initiated by a well-known telecommunications company. The company had identified 250 call-center employees who worked in the New Orleans area. They traced employees' cell phone signals to triangulate their positions, and then they ran rescue missions to bring employees and their families to safety. After finding the last employee and her ten family members, who had been trapped in a second-story apartment, a meeting was called. About 100 people filled the conference room, including executive team members and several families that had been brought to safety.

The CEO took the podium to speak. "Over the last few days we have broken some rules here," he said. "We have cut through the red tape and pulled out all the stops. Well, I think I'll break just one more rule."

He then reached into his pocket and pulled out a Bible, at which point he began to read the parable of the lost sheep from Matthew 18:

> *What do you think? If a man owns a hundred sheep, and one of them wanders away, will he not leave the ninety-nine on the hills and go to look for the one that wandered off? And if he finds it, I tell you the truth, he is happier about that one sheep than about the ninety-nine that did not wander off. In the same way your Father in Heaven is not willing that any of these little ones should be lost* (Matthew 18:12-14).

The executive then looked at the family of 11 people they had just rescued and compassionately said, "You were the lost sheep, and we were not going home without you."

## SHOW YOU CARE

Compassion reveals itself when we show others that we care. More than any other quality, compassion sets the tone for serving others. We may say we care. We may even act like we care. However, compassion reveals the true feelings of our hearts. Compassion truly moves us to care about serving others.

My company is blessed with many outstanding employees. Each top performer is unique and brings certain distinct strengths and abilities to our team. Though these exceptional employees differ in many ways, they all possess the quality of compassion. Typically the best employees in any setting are those who genuinely care for others and express that care by serving.

Instinctively, we all long to be cared for. It's amazing how customers will keep coming back when they know that we care. Conversely, a lack of compassion can cost any business dearly. Research by the American Society for Quality and the Quality and Productivity Center shows that 68 percent of customers who take their business elsewhere do so because they were turned away by an attitude of indifference on the part of the prior service provider.[1]

Smart business people understand the important role that serving others plays in gaining or losing customers. The same holds true for employees. The most coveted work environment is one where employees are cared for, appreciated, and empowered to make a difference. When employees know that they are valued and cared for, they in turn will value and care for customers. In business and in life, compassion manifests itself when we cast aside our own selfish ambitions and genuinely desire our service to be a blessing to others, regardless of the potential return.

Sound overwhelming? Here's a little secret: Showing someone we care is not terribly difficult if we really do care. "Be kindly affectionate to one another with brotherly love, in honor giving preference to one another" (Rom. 12:10 NKJV). If you encounter someone who has a need, don't just point them in a particular direction or try to pass them off on someone else. Rather, do your best to understand and help them, or personally lead them somewhere that their need can be served. Often those we serve gain comfort by knowing that we care enough to try and help them. That's why so many problems smooth out almost instantly when we really tune in to someone else's situation. Most problems are solved not by those who have all the answers but by those who show they care.

---

**Most problems are solved by those who show they care.**

---

## KNOW YOU CARE

If we serve others just because we have to, it will show. We cannot counterfeit compassion. Caring about the welfare of another requires an attitude of the heart that shines through in every facet of our being. If we have true compassion, people will:

- See it.
- Feel it.
- Know it.

Think about a time you received poor service from someone. More than likely, that person left you with the impression that they just did not care. A study by Daniel Yankolovich revealed that two-thirds of customers do not feel valued by those serving them.[2] Obviously the heart of compassion is commonly lacking in today's workplace.

Many years ago, I witnessed, right in one of my own stores, one of the worst examples of service I have ever seen. A customer walked in the door and received no greeting. He walked over to our parts counter where our customer service representative was busy on the computer. After pounding the keys for what seemed like an eternity, without even looking up, our employee muttered, "Can I help you?"

---

**Others know we care only when we show we care.**

---

As the customer began to explain what he needed, the phone rang. Our employee cut the customer off mid-sentence by grabbing the phone and screaming into the receiver, "Parts!" The customer then stood there and waited until the phone call was concluded.

Not much compassion in that example. However, before you get too judgmental, think about how often each of us is guilty of similar behavior. Has your child ever rambled on about something only to end up asking, "Are you listening to me?" Has your spouse ever tried to talk to you while you have been preoccupied watching television or reading?

## BE PRESENT

"When I first came to work here, I did not like you. I thought you were aloof and stuck up. You walked around barely noticing and rarely paying attention to anyone. But now that I have been here a while, I know you're not that bad. Now I know you really do care about others. Because you always have other things on your mind, you just don't always show it."

I did not know how to respond when a young employee enlightened me with this information a few years back. She was trying to give me a compliment. But it sure did not feel like one.

I am a dreamer and a focused thinker. If not mindful, I can get all wrapped up in my own world and miss all that moves, breathes, and happens around me. Truthfully, I really do care about others. I just don't show it often enough. It is my desire that each employee would know that I care about them. But this doesn't happen automatically. It requires deliberate empathy.

Empathy is the ability to enter into, to understand, and to share someone else's feelings. If we want others to know that we care, it is our responsibility to show that we care. Most people will not stick around long to find out if we really do care. They generally make that decision rather quickly. Compassion often requires that we put our own thoughts on hold and simply be there for someone.

The best way to reveal empathy is to listen intently. This is harder than it sounds because listening is so much more than hearing. We have to draw out the deeper meaning when others talk to us. The following are some techniques that can help:

**Engage.** Look them in the eyes, and give them your full attention. Repeat things, ask for clarification, and reveal genuine interest. This assures that you hear what they say. It also keeps you focused.

**Be open-minded.** Put your own opinions and biases on hold so that you can fully understand the other person. This helps you draw them out more, as well as preparing you to better express your own viewpoint when the time comes.

**Wait.** Do not guess at their meaning, cut them short, or finish sentences for them. Listening is about them, not you. The more they say, the more you can learn.

**Connect.** The best way to connect with the heart is by opening your ears. By listening with empathy, you enable their words to affect you and to connect with you on the heart level.

**Be flexible.** You must be willing to change your mind, if necessary. This does not mean that you have to let go of your values or turn off your brain. However, you need to be less defensive and more open to adjusting your opinion—based on the information you get from others.

This kind of listening happens only when we are genuinely compassionate and willing to be present for someone. It requires that we put all other things on hold and give people our full attention.

## DO SOMETHING

Compassion requires more than just a feeling of empathy. We must express our concern through action. We can listen, understand, and show empathy. But until we do something about it, we have not shown how much we care. James 2:17 tells us that faith without works is dead. But concern without action is not worth much either.

How often do we say, "I'll pray for you," and then walk away without taking any further action? Although we definitely should follow through by praying, authentic compassion often requires that we go beyond just praying. To demonstrate true compassion, we should follow the model of Jesus:

> *Two blind men sitting by the road, when they heard that Jesus was passing by, cried out, saying, "Have mercy on us, O Lord, Son of David!"... Jesus stood still and called them, and said, "What do you want Me to do for you?" They said to Him, "Lord, that our eyes may be opened." So Jesus had compassion and touched their eyes. And immediately their eyes received sight, and they followed Him* (Matthew 20:30-34 NKJV).

Notice what Jesus asked the two blind men in the passage above: "What do you want me to do for you?" He knew what they needed; still, He asked the question.

A great question to ask those we serve is: "What can I do for you?" Asking the question communicates our concern, and hearing their need provides the specific opportunity to respond with compassion. If it is within our power to meet that need, we should do it. Like Christ, we should connect with others, feel their pain, and do what we can to help.

## FOLLOW UP

One of the simplest ways to show we care is to follow up with someone to see how they are doing. If a fellow employee has shared something with us, our following up with them makes the strong statement that we really do care. If we recently have served a customer, a quick call or note to check on that customer goes a long way. At a minimum, we should ask:

- Was our service a good value for you?
- Did we live up to our promises?
- Would you recommend our service to others?
- How can we serve you better in the future?

Follow-up provides an opportunity to see how our service is playing out. It is also an opportunity to find out how we might better serve them in the future. Most importantly, follow-up clearly communicates how much we care.

The formula for showing compassion is simple:

- Ask.
- Listen.
- Empathize.
- Take action.
- Follow up.

Whether it's lending a hand, lending an ear, or lending support, do what you can to help improve someone else's situation.

---

**Endnotes**

1. Lisa Ford, David McNair, Bill Perry, *Exceptional Customer Service* (Holbrook, MA: Adams Media Corp, 2001), 6.
2. Ibid, 7.

## Chapter 4

# Shine With Generosity

### EXCEED EXPECTATIONS

*Whoever sows sparingly will also reap sparingly, and whoever sows generously will also reap generously* (2 Corinthians 9:6).

The incredible enthusiasm and generous service of a busboy helped me to better process the SHINE vision. I was having dinner with some colleagues when, in my opinion, the best busboy in the world began to clear the table next to us. He had focus, a well thought-out plan, and unparalleled enthusiasm. He also flawlessly executed his task. In fact, never in the history of food service has anyone more efficiently turned a dirty table into a clean set-up, ready for the next guest.

I could not stop watching this busboy as he worked—putting on the same sparkling demonstration time after time. Others were watching too, for eventually the entire restaurant would erupt, right on cue, whenever he finished a table. That night, I could not sleep after witnessing that server at work. The image of the world's greatest busboy would not leave my mind. But more than that, I found myself wondering if anyone would ever applaud me for the work I do. Would anyone ever pause to say, "Here lived a tractor salesman who did his job well"?

Then I really began to dream—imagining applause every time I spoke to an employee or served a customer because of the excellent service I had rendered. I envisioned my entire company performing so well that it would glow from the sheer radiance of its own achievements.

I have never actually heard God's audible voice. But, at that moment, I felt as if He spoke directly to my heart. It was time to make some adjustments in my service. God revealed that my efforts could indeed shine, though not for my own applause. However, through His works done in and through me, others would applaud Him. Scripture instructs us:

> *Arise, shine; for your light has come! And the glory of the Lord is risen upon you. For behold, the darkness shall cover the earth, and deep darkness the people; but the Lord will arise over you, and His glory will be seen upon you* (Isaiah 60:1-2 NKJV).

## EXCEED EXPECTATIONS

Martin Luther King, Jr. said,

> If a man is called to be a street sweeper, he should sweep streets even as Michelangelo painted, or Beethoven composed music, or Shakespeare wrote poetry. He should sweep streets so well that all the hosts of Heaven and earth will pause to say, "Here lived a street sweeper who did his job well."[1]

Have you ever received such exceptional service that it was worthy of applause? Ponder for a moment the last time you received outstanding service that completely exceeded your expectations. Often those instances are difficult to recall.

Now think about the last time you received poor service. That should be easier to recall. I once read that the average customer will remember an outstanding service incident for about 18 months but will remember a poor one for about 23.5 years. What a disparity! The fact is that nobody remembers normal service. Average service never receives applause.

Thankfully, the ability to provide generous service is fully under our own control. Often opportunities to serve present themselves disguised as problems. It is important to realize that people with problems or concerns are not looking for someone to blame. They are searching for someone to serve their need. Often we look to place blame on things we have no control over instead of offering rectifying service in the areas we can control. Making excuses or blaming someone else never leads to exceeding expectations.

For example, as an equipment dealer, my company cannot control the quality or the design of the products we offer. That responsibility falls on the manufacturer. However, we do control the level of support and customer service we deliver. If a piece of equipment fails, our blaming the manufacturer doesn't help anybody feel better. Nobody cares who's to blame for the failure. They just want their equipment to work again for them. Since we cannot control the quality of the product, we focus our effort on what we can control: service to our customer.

In our industry, the key question has shifted from "What's the best product?" to "Who can provide the best service?" Consumers today have so many choices of quality products. Accordingly, the product itself has become less important. And something entirely new has come into play. Research shows that, in many industries, consumer buying decisions are based approximately ten percent on quality of product and 90 percent on quality of service. This trend is great news for the servant-hearted company because the level of service we provide to others is fully under our own control.

---

**We serve others because God called us to serve.**

---

Obviously, the businesses which gain the greatest competitive advantages in the future will be those who serve generously. Employees who serve generously will make the biggest impact. Yet, before we can serve generously, we need to understand the difference between serving and pleasing others. Serving generously does not mean trying to make everybody happy. We don't serve others to please them; we serve others because God has called us to serve. Serving with generosity means giving our best for all parties involved. It is taking responsibility to serve the Lord by serving others. Therefore, our goal is not to please people but to serve as God has instructed. To take our service to the highest level we should serve as though we are serving Him personally.

> *Whatever you do, work at it with all your heart, as working for the Lord, not for men* (Colossians 3:23).

The self-serving employee who just wants to get by will seldom be valued very highly. But an employee who serves generously honors God and increases his value to his employer, his customers, and himself. Art Linkletter said, "Do a little more than you're paid to. Give a little more than you have to. Try a little harder than you want to. Aim a little higher than you think possible. And give a lot of thanks to God for health, family, and friends."[2]

## SERVE UNCONDITIONALLY

Serving generously requires that we take the initiative to serve. We cannot sit around at our desks waiting for an opportunity to come find us. Do not wait for a better time. Take the opportunity to step out and engage someone, serve their need, and make a positive impact. It's good for us, good for others, and it's good for business. Proactively initiating service without requirement is the first step toward exceeding expectations.

Generous service goes beyond what we are paid to do. It is a choice we make to provide more than what is expected of us. Generous service is never selective service. Someone's position, station in life, or relative importance should not matter. Along those lines, it is easy to serve people we know and like but much harder to serve those we don't. Likewise, it's easy to serve when we anticipate a reward and not so easy when we see no obvious benefit. And yet, if we are to serve generously, we must be willing to serve anyone, without arbitrary judgments.

My dad tells a story that illustrates this pretty well. It had been a long week, and he was ready to head home to the family. But on his way to his car, he met a middle-aged gentleman wearing grungy clothes and driving a beat-up truck. The fellow said he wanted to look at a tree-transplanting machine for a local project. Based on this man's appearance, my dad assumed he would waste his time. However, he took the man into the equipment yard and hurriedly rushed through a presentation. The fellow seemed impressed. He told my dad he would arrange to buy a machine on Monday. "I'll never see that guy again," my dad thought as he drove home that night.

And he was right. He never did see the same person again. But, first thing on Monday morning, he did see a property manager, who brought him a check for a new tree-transplanting machine. In conversation with the property manager, my dad came to realize that the gentleman who he had helped on Friday night was Kemmons Wilson, the founder of Holiday Inn. Mr. Wilson bought the tree-transplanting machine for a large development project of his.

Generous service pays no attention to perceived status. A great way to think about this is to remember that we will never meet anybody who doesn't matter to God. He cares for us all.

> *Live in harmony with each other. Don't be too proud to enjoy the company of ordinary people.... Do things in such a way that everyone can see you are honorable* (Romans 12:16-17 NLT).

## GO THE EXTRA MILE

When Jesus walked the earth, His people were governed by Roman law. During this period of history, Roman soldiers could demand the Israelites to drop what they were doing and serve them, by carrying their equipment for one mile, at any time. It was the law. Understandably, this law was not popular among the people. They saw it as one more visible sign of their oppression under Roman rule.

Jesus, however, took a totally different perspective. Instead of complaining, He exhorted His followers to do more than what the law required:

"If someone forces you to go one mile, go with him two miles" (Matt. 5:41). In other words, always exceed expectations. Imagine the potential impact when we, rather than begrudgingly serving the minimum requirement, generously choose to perform beyond the expectation.

Too often today, we view our work as just another sign of our own oppression. That is why some people quickly establish the lowest acceptable standards for performing their jobs—doing just enough to squeeze by. For example, many of us have thought or said:

- *It's the same old job, just a different day.*
- *It's not my problem; someone else is to blame.*
- *They don't pay me enough to do that.*
- *It's not my job; let someone else do it.*
- *Nobody even appreciates what I do.*
- *I can't believe they expect that of me.*

These kinds of statements all describe first-mile thinking. They come from the depths of self-pity and reveal a hapless "I'm oppressed" mind-set. Yet, Jesus calls us to go beyond the minimum standards. He calls us to rise above the attitude of oppression, to stop worrying about what's fair, and to focus on what's right. The first mile is focused on self and what we must do to survive in our work. The first mile is doing what's expected. The second mile is focused on going above and beyond expectations to serve generously. The second mile is exceeding expectations. It is on the second mile that we shine at work. Second-mile statements are more like:

- *This is a great opportunity to serve.*
- *I'm sorry that happened to you; how can I help?*
- *Thank you for this opportunity; I appreciate it very much.*
- *I will do my best to serve your need.*
- *What else can I do for you?*
- *How can I serve you better in the future?*

## DON'T HOLD BACK

In the book, *The Generosity Factor,* Kenneth Blanchard and S. Truett Cathy write: "A lot of folks say they care about people, but they don't actually do anything about it. Generosity is all about caring about the needs of others, then acting to meet those needs . . . about balance . . . about making all of one's resources available."[3]

Generosity reflects our efforts to give our all from the depths of our hearts. Even so, we are often misled by seemingly valid excuses. Maybe we don't feel well, have other things on our minds, or don't see eye-to-eye with the boss. Countless distractions get in the way. However, we must rise above excuses and challenges. When we realize that we are working for God and not for man, it becomes a lot easier to find the motivation to rise above and give our best effort.

---

**We can give our best effort when we realize we work for God and not for man.**

---

A helpful practice is to visualize God watching our every move as we carry out our duties. That should kick up our enthusiasm a bit! As followers of Christ, we should be serving Him with generosity, regardless of personal circumstance. As we radiate God's generous grace, the impact reaches far beyond our own efforts. Then our aim becomes the eventual greatness found in serving others—the generosity of putting more into life than we take out. We serve others through generosity. Exceed expectations.

---

### Endnotes

1. Martin Luther King, Jr., www.quotationspage.com (accessed 15 November 2007).

2. Mark Victor Hansen and Joe Batten, *The Master Motivator* (Deerfield Beach, FL: Health communications, Inc., 1995), 70.

3. Kenneth H. Blanchard and S. Truett Cathy, *The Generosity Factor* (Grand Rapids, MI: Zondervan, 2002), 43.

## Reflection

# My Mission of Service

### SUMMARY

**Principle One: Serve Others**

One of the keys to shining beyond significance is to seek a clearly articulated mission focused on serving others. My company's mission is "to earn recommendations by serving with integrity." This requires a focus on serving so completely that others would recommend our service to someone else. Regrettably, we often fall short and sometimes stray from our mission. However, the mission clearly defines our intention and helps keep us on the right track. When we know what our mission is, we are more likely to achieve success in our own eyes and in the eyes of others. A mission of service permits us to evaluate ourselves against a set measure and prevents us from pursuing things that would distract us from our goals.

The beauty of servanthood is that anyone can serve a mission. Servanthood does not require a fancy title, an array of knowledge, or vast experience. It simply shines through a servant's heart. Scripture tells us, "The greatest among you will be your servant" (Matt. 23:11).

**Application**

1. Who do you serve with your work?
2. How could you improve your service to others?
3. What can you do in your work place to model these qualities?
    a. Humility

   b. Compassion
   c. Generosity
4. How can God use you to serve others at work?

**Think about it:**

What is your mission of service?

## CORE VALUE STATEMENT

***A heart of servanthood glorifies God by helping others.***

# Principle Two

# HONOR GOD

*But seek first His Kingdom and His righteousness, and all these things will be given to you as well*
**(Matthew 6:33).**

# Chapter 5

# Ignite the Flame of Faithfulness

## A SOUL OF FAITHFULNESS OBEYS GOD'S PURPOSE

*Let love and faithfulness never leave you; bind them around your neck, write them on the tablet of your heart* (Proverbs 3:3).

We recently asked some members of our sales team to describe a personal role model who has highly impacted their lives. One of the most interesting ones came from a young man named Curt, who chose his former college football coach, Ron Schipper, a football legend. As head coach at Central College in Pella, Iowa, he racked up 287 wins and 18 conference championships. Beyond these achievements, this outstanding coach is remembered for much more than his win-loss record. CBS news anchor Harry Smith recounted:

> In the world of college football, he was a pretty big deal. He was one of the most successful coaches who ever lived. He had a record 36 consecutive winning seasons. The minute he retired, he went straight into the College Football Hall of Fame. You've never heard of him because he was a small college coach. NCAA Division III, where there are no scholarships, no slush funds, and no scandals. He was a legend in that world . . . He was tough and old fashioned. Schipper knew more about football than just about any coach in the

> country, but here was the difference: He loved us, his players, unconditionally. I'm convinced that's why we won.[1]

The bigger schools would call him with offers of more money, greater exposure, and increased opportunity. Yet, Schipper always remained at Central. For this old ball coach, the purpose of his work stretched beyond personal ambition and focused on positively impacting the lives of others. He passionately coached his players to be gentlemen, students, and athletes . . . in that order. At Schipper's memorial service in April of 2006, past Central College president Dr. Kenneth Weller recalled:

> Ron Schipper has always been one of those "bigger than life" people. He still is! He lives on in an immense assemblage of people who in their younger years were inspired by his intelligence, his emotion, his ideals and deep concern for each of them. The wellspring of his phenomenal success as a coach, a teacher, and a person lies in the fact he was always a giver, not a taker.[2]

Curt played in Schipper's final game in 1996, a win to cap off a stellar career. As the media, fans, and other players left the stadium, Curt returned to search for something he'd left behind. What he ended up finding was his Hall of Fame coach cleaning up the muddy visitor's locker room with paper towels.

Coach Schipper's faithfulness still inspires Curt to this day: "He loved his job. He was passionate about making each of us better people. He exemplified it's not all about glory and recognition, but about consistently doing the right things for the right reasons. His commitment to excellence rubbed off on everyone who came in contact with him. He was one of the most faithful men I have ever known."

## FAITHFUL PEOPLE

Faithfulness is a character quality not often linked to the workplace. When the term faithful is used at work, it is often misunderstood. For years I have traveled to our various locations to discuss employee performance with our local store managers. I love to hear how people are doing and discuss how we can help them improve. Once an operations manager referred to a particular employee as an underperforming, poor-quality worker with a really negative attitude. The manager went on to explain that he'd done everything possible to help this employee succeed, but had seen no improvement. The next statement really floored me, "But he is probably one of the most faithful employees I have ever had." To this manager, faithfulness meant that one had been around a while and always showed up for work. Obviously, faithfulness requires much more than that.

It is true; showing up every day is a good idea. A faithful employee, however, should also be trustworthy and reliable—someone who can be counted on to get the job done right. Faithful employees are loyal, dependable, dedicated, and committed to giving their best effort, regardless of circumstance. They do the right things for the right reasons. Faithful employees positively impact an organization through their positive example of faithfulness.

At the same time, faithful employers should be fair, just, and care deeply for the employees of an organization. They should always deliver what they promise. Faithful employers are committed to high standards of performance, help employees improve, and cultivate a culture of honesty and ethical morality. Faithful employers do not tolerate behavior that contradicts the values and culture of the organization. They commit to correcting unsatisfactory behavior and, ultimately, to improving or removing it from the organization. Faithfulness requires strict adherence to the principles and values to which an organization believes are most important.

## FAITHFUL PROVIDER

Faithfulness is used often in the Bible as a description of God: ". . . You are mighty, O Lord, and Your faithfulness surrounds You" (Ps. 89:8). God's faithfulness is mentioned over 30 times alone in the book of Psalms. Every aspect of a believer's life is anchored in the faithfulness of a God who has never failed us.

> *Your Kingdom is an everlasting kingdom, and your dominion endures through all generations. The Lord is faithful to all His promises and loving toward all He has made* (Psalm 145:13).

So to whom should we pledge our faithfulness? Is it our boss, our company, the code of ethics, the board of directors? Sometimes employers don't even stand for the ideals we value. Sometimes we may view our work as insignificant and not worthy of faithfulness. These are just some of the reasons faithfulness is not all that common in the workplace. Yet, Scripture tells us: "If you are faithful in little things, you will be faithful in large ones . . . " (Luke 16:10 NLT). Regardless of who our boss is, where we work, or what job we hold, God still desires faithfulness in all we do. He continually develops our faithfulness in the small things so that He can use us for much more important things.

---

**God isn't looking for people who just show up.**

---

John Trent said, "Imagine getting up in the morning not dreading but dedicated to going to work for a purpose—His purpose for you in your workplace! You may never change the entire corporate culture where you work, but you can change lives—your own and many others as well."[3]

God isn't looking for people who just show up. He's looking for those He can count on to build His Kingdom and make Him known through all the earth. He wants us to honor Him in all we do. God's Spirit dwells in the faithful and empowers them to accomplish His purposes. God is faithful to provide for all of the needs of those who follow Him.

> *My eyes will be on the faithful in the land that they may dwell with Me . . .* (Psalm 101:6).

## FAITHFUL POWER

If you are like me, you probably question how your work could possibly honor and glorify God. I spent years struggling with this concept. Eventually, I cried out in prayer, "What do you want from me God? I'm only a tractor salesman. I'm not qualified to build your Kingdom. How could I possibly honor you with the work I do?" At that point, God began to reveal an astonishing truth to me: He does not call the equipped to do His work. He equips those He calls so that He can work in and through them. It doesn't matter how qualified we are, what we do for a living, or where we attend church. It is our calling to love Him, obey Him, and seek Him with heart, soul, mind, and strength. It is through this faithfulness that God works in us and reveals Himself: "For it is God who works in you to will and to act according to His good purpose" (Phil. 2:13). It's not what we do for God that honors Him. It is what He does through us that brings Him glory.

---

**It's not what we do for God, but what He does through us that brings Him glory.**

---

It's hard for me to fathom why God would choose to work through ordinary individuals like us to accomplish His purposes. But that is exactly what He does! Throughout time, God has done, and continues to do, extraordinary works through ordinary people who are faithful to Him. God places a burning desire in our hearts to do His will. He then equips us for the journey of faith. When honoring God is our soul's true motivation, we are empowered to fulfill a purpose of faithfulness. Agnes Bojaxhiu—a simple social worker better known as Mother Teresa—said:

> "I am nothing. He is all. I do nothing of my own. He does it. I am God's pencil. A tiny bit of pencil with which He writes what He likes. God writes through us, and however imperfect instruments we may be, He writes beautifully."[4]

## FAITHFUL PURPOSE

As we honor our relationship with God, He works in us and carries out His purposes through us. We don't have to be a pastor, a missionary, or the president of a company in order to honor Him with our work. The Bible calls all believers a "royal priesthood" (see 1 Pet. 2:9). Regardless of our profession or position, we are all called to ministry as our work provides opportunity to faithfully serve these godly purposes:

- Honor God.
- Reflect God's glory.
- Provide for others' needs.
- Build God's Kingdom.

---

**A soul of faithfulness obeys God's purpose.**

---

Souls of faithfulness honor God by revealing *trust* in Him, through *gratitude* glorifying Him, and by *stewardship* meeting needs as He builds His Kingdom through us. By faithfulness, God equips us to accomplish His purpose to advance His Kingdom both here and forever. Scripture reminds us that God's master purpose will always be accomplished: "Many are the plans in a man's heart, but it is the Lord's purpose that prevails" (Prov. 19:21).

### Endnotes

1. Harry Smith, "Opinion," www.cbsnews.com (accessed 31 March 2006).
2. Kenneth Weller, quoted in "Football Archive," www.central.edu (accessed 27 March 2006).
3. John Trent, quoted in William Nix, *Transforming Your Workplace for Christ* (Nashville, TN: Broadman & Holman Publishers, 1997), xii.
4. Mother Teresa, quoted in "Mother Teresa Autobiography," www.comcast.net (accessed March 2006).

## Chapter 6

# Shine With Trust

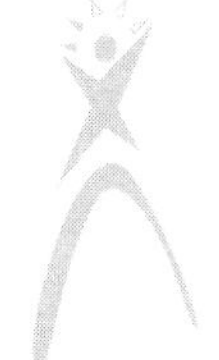

### DEPEND ON HIM

*Trust in the Lord with all your heart and lean not on your own understanding; in all your ways acknowledge Him, and He will make your paths straight* (Proverbs 3:5-6).

The story is told that, at a little church in the country, one Sunday morning, a visitor, an old friend of the pastor, stepped up to the pulpit to speak: "True story," he began. "A father took his son and a friend of his son sailing off the Pacific Coast. It was a marvelous time, until suddenly the weather changed. A mighty storm came upon them before they could make it back to shore, and a giant wave swept the two boys into the ocean."

The old man made eye contact with a teenager who was, for the first time since the service began, looking somewhat interested in what was happening. "Grabbing a rescue line, the father knew that only one boy could be saved. He did not have time to think. Facing into the wind, hoping his words would be heard, he yelled, 'I love you, son!' and flung that line into the hands of his son's friend. By the time he pulled the friend back to the boat, his son had disappeared, never to be seen again."

The teenager sat straighter in the pew, waiting for the next words to come out of the old man's mouth. "When they finally made it back to shore, the friend was weeping. 'Why?' he demanded. 'Why did you save me instead of him?'

Tears were streaming down the father's face, as well, but he smiled. 'My son has stepped into eternity with Jesus. If you had died, you would have missed the opportunity to give your life to Christ.'

How great is the love of God that He should do the same for us. Don't waste your opportunity." With that, the old man turned and sat back down in his chair as silence filled the room. After the service ended, the teenager rushed to the old man's side. "That can't be a true story," started the boy. "No father would give up his son's life in hopes that the other boy would become a Christian. That'd be crazy!"

The old man smiled. "Crazy but true," he said. "You see, I was that father, and your pastor was my son's friend."[1]

## GODLY TRUST

The old man in this story unreservedly put his trust in God and His plan for salvation. This trust clearly is evidenced through his actions. It is true that we may never face such an excruciating choice as this. Yet, in less dramatic ways, we do make choices that reflect where our trust lies. Our daily lives constantly reveal this.

It is so easy to place our trust in the wrong things at work. We place our trust in money, power, prestige, and position. Quickly we find ourselves pursuing our own strategies and roadmaps to succeed. We put pressure on ourselves to advance, stand out, and strive for achievement. Excellence, high performance, and hard work are all worthy goals. Yet, more important than reaching these goals is how we choose to get there. Do we trust in our own power, or do we trust in God? The author of Proverbs wrote, "Commit to the Lord whatever you do, and your plans will succeed" (Prov. 16:3). Scripture is clear about whom we should trust—confidence in God over reliance on self—and how we should strive to succeed. Our personal and professional goals should be focused on doing life and work God's way by trusting in His plan and relying on His power.

Still, I often choose to trust in my own strength rather than in God's power. In my small company, over 200 employees are counting on me and trusting in my leadership to guide us to enduring success. At times, this responsibility energizes me, and at other times, the stress takes it toll. One day I was agonizing over a situation, and one of our managers walked in and shut the door behind him. "Something's weighing on you, Kris," he said. "How can I help?"

"I wish you could," I told him. "But there really is nothing you could do." I mustered up as much bravado as possible and tried to assure him he did not need to worry. "As the leader of the organization, I will deal with this situation myself."

We chatted a bit longer. And then he got up to walk out of the room. However, before he left, he caught my eye and said, "You are confident in God, and for that reason alone, I am confident in you. I trust you because I know you trust Him."

This manager reminded me that the confidence others place in me is directly related to the confidence I—and they—place in God. When we trust in Him, it relieves the stress we place on ourselves. We honor God by placing our confident hope in Him to provide the best outcome: "Those who hope in the Lord will renew their strength. They will soar on wings like eagles . . . " (Isa. 40:31).

## EARNED TRUST

Trust is the foundation of all successful relationships. It is also the foundation of all successful organizations. Trust is not an entitlement but a virtue that is established over time. Our actions continually are evaluated by those we interact with to determine our level of trustworthiness. As trust grows, opportunity and responsibility also grow with it.

A primary role of leadership is to develop a high level of trust within the organization. Accordingly, the enduring success of an organization is built on the trustworthiness of its leaders. Likewise, trusted employees are most likely to receive promotions and greater opportunity. Customers strongly desire to do business with people they trust.

I once had a notoriously demanding customer call to discuss his feelings about one of our service managers. He said, "Nobody makes me angrier than your service manager. He never tells me what I want to hear. He never budges to any of my demands. But he always comes through with what he promises. Most people tell me what I want to hear and then let me down. But not him. I can't say I really like him much, but I certainly respect him. He's earned my trust. That's why I keep coming back for more."

A great way to earn trust is:

1. Do what you say.
2. Do it when you say you'll do it.
3. Do it right the first time.
4. Always under-promise and over-deliver.

---

**To move ahead in your faith, trust God.**

---

Once trust is earned, loyalty results. One of the greatest compliments anyone can receive is in hearing the words, "I trust you." Similarly, we express our love for God through actions that reveal our trust in Him. God blesses those who trust Him. In fact, the more we trust in God, the more He entrusts to us. God expects faithfulness from us: "Now it is required that those who have been given a trust must prove faithful" (1 Cor. 4:2). The more we step out in trusting obedience, the more faithful we become—and the more loyal we are proven.

## OBEDIENT TRUST

If you want to move ahead in your work, be a person worthy of trust. If you want to move ahead in your faith, trust God. The key to establishing and maintaining trust is found in unyielding obedience to God and His will. Trust and obedience go hand in hand. Trust confirms our internal beliefs and fortifies our faith. Obedience reveals this faith through the external behavior evidenced in our works. To obey God, we must first trust Him. Trust in God reveals what we believe about Him. When we accept Jesus, we trust in His way—and in His way alone: "I am the way and the truth and the life. No one comes to the Father except through Me (John 14:6).

God shows His unconditional love for us through the salvation we find in Jesus Christ. In turn, when we commit to Jesus, we show our love for God through obedient lives centered on Him.

In *Experiencing God,* Henry Blackaby compares a self-centered life to a God-centered life:[2]

| SELF-CENTERED | GOD-CENTERED |
|---|---|
| Life focused on self | Life focused on God |
| Pride in self and self's own accomplishments | Humbleness before God |
| Self-confidence | Confidence in God |
| Depending on self and self's own abilities | Dependence on God, His ability and provision |
| Affirming self | Denying self |
| Seeking to be acceptable to the world and its ways | Seeking first the Kingdom of God and His righteousness |
| Looking at circumstances from a human perspective | Seeking God's perspective in every circumstance |
| Selfish and ordinary living | Holy and godly living |

How would you describe your life at work? Is it self-centered or is it God-centered? When our lives reveal trust in and obedience to Him, we become available for God to work in us to accomplish His purposes for His glory.

## RELIANT TRUST

We demonstrate our trust in God when we bow to Him in prayer. Never are we more in touch with God's power than when we are on our knees in prayer. We can confidently rely on Him as our source of help and strength: "I lift up my eyes to the hills—where does my help come from? My help comes from the Lord, the Maker of Heaven and earth" (Ps. 121:1-2).

I used to pray for specific outcomes from God for my business. I would think about what I wanted, and then I would pray that God would provide it. I have come to learn that this is a very limiting and selfish type of prayer. The outcomes we desire pale in comparison to God's plans.

A few years ago, one of our top sales reps was offered a sales manager position by another company. I feared the thought of losing this employee since he brought great value to our company. As I began to pray that God would make him stay, it became clear that my prayer was inappropriate. Instead, I needed to trust in God to provide for our company and pray His will be done for our employee. I began to pray this way and to trust in God for the best outcome.

> *But when I am afraid, I put my trust in You. I praise God for what He has promised. I trust in God, so why should I be afraid . . .* (Psalm 56:3-4 NLT).

This employee agonized for weeks over the decision. It was difficult for me to refrain from persuading him to stay. One afternoon over the phone, I suggested that God only knows what this decision should be, and asked if I could pray for him. He said it was okay, so I prayed, "God, you are in control of all aspects of our lives. You are in control of this difficult decision. I trust you will make your way known. Let your will be done on earth as it is in Heaven."

The next morning, our employee informed me that he would be leaving. While thanking him for his efforts, a strong leading overcame me to discuss salvation with him. As uncomfortable as the timing was, I blurted out, "I'm not nearly as concerned about where you spend the next few years working as about where you will spend eternity." I explained my trust in Jesus, my belief in eternal life, and my desire to see this employee in Heaven some day. He grew increasingly uncomfortable. He jumped up and proclaimed, "I have to go," and swiftly left my office.

A few days later, he called to inform me about his change of heart. He explained that his mother had been praying for him to find Jesus. She had mentioned to her pastor the difficult work decision her son was facing. The pastor committed to pray. A few days later, the pastor had called and said, "I really think your son needs to stay where he is. I feel he is where God wants him to be." This pastor was over 1300 miles away and knew little about our company. He just felt led to share this counsel as he had been praying for God's guidance in this situation. The employee stayed with our company, and he has since grown into management and leadership within our organization. More importantly, God used that time in his life and work to bring him into a relationship with Jesus.

---

**Honor God with trust. Depend on Him.**

---

Sometimes the greatest thing we can do for someone is simply to lift their name in prayer. It continues to amaze me what God does when we trust Him and leave the outcome to Him. When we trust God, He removes the stress that we place on ourselves. We no longer place our trust in money, power, people, or other resources. Instead, we trust in almighty God, the provider of all resources and relationships. And by trusting God, we too become trustworthy.

## Endnotes

1. Original source of this story is unknown.
2. Henry Blackaby and Claude V. King, *Experiencing God* (Nashville, TN: Broadman & Holman, 1994), 100-101.

# Chapter 7

# Shine With Gratitude

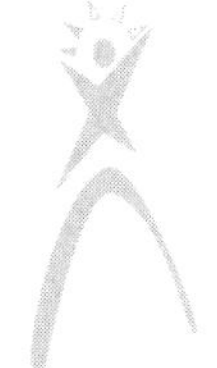

## GLORIFY HIM

*We should be grateful that we were given a kingdom that cannot be shaken. And in this kingdom we please God by worshiping Him and by showing Him great honor and respect*
(Hebrews 12:28 CEV).

Monte joined our company straight out of college. An Iowa farm boy with a strong work ethic and extreme ambition, he quickly became one of our top sales representatives. It's been a blessing to see him grow, both personally and professionally, over the years. He currently serves as our director of sales training. The following letter clearly expresses his gratitude for work:

> Kris,
>
> I woke up this morning at about 3:30 A.M. with this message weighing on my heart, and I want to share it with you. I have to admit, when you first rolled out our new vision statement, "To Shine with Excellence," at the Christmas party a few years back, I truly felt it would become just like most of the other vision statements from companies . . . a catchy phrase with no buy-in from the people.

Well, I am thankful to say I could not have been more wrong. To watch the growth of our company since God planted that vision with you has been incredible. The neat thing is, when I say growth, I don't just mean the type of growth that is measured by profit at the end of the year (although that has happened, too). I am talking about the personal and spiritual growth of the employees of this company. Not only have I experienced it, I have witnessed it in the lives of many others.

When I came to this company straight out of college, there was one thing that drove me . . . MONEY! That's it. I'm thankful my work now counts for more than that.

Most importantly I have come to know Jesus Christ as my personal Lord and Savior. It's one thing to hear about Christ on Sunday, but to see his principles lived out in the work place is a very powerful testimony and one that had a big impact on my eventual decision to follow Him. Thank you for allowing God to work through you to create that culture here.

In addition, SHINE has brought a renewed passion and fulfillment to my work life. It has allowed me to connect the "what I do" with the "why I do it." Now I realize that God has a purpose for all of us. I know that God has placed me right where I am for a reason.

I'm thankful to work at a place that I am allowed to open our sales meetings in prayer. For many of our employees, this is the only time they even hear a prayer. I know God is using that time to plant seeds.

There are numerous other ways SHINE has impacted me and those around me. Bottom line is though, I'm grateful God has allowed me to be part of this company. I am truly blessed.

Your friend,
Monte

## GRATEFUL THOUGHTS

Many people consider work to be like a game or battlefield—an opportunity for advancement. For them, pride and ego are built around personal achievement and making more money. To others, work is a curse, a rat race, or just a necessary evil. Seldom do we hear work described as a blessing.

We are much more apt to brag about personal accomplishment or grumble about work than we are to express gratitude and thankfulness for it. We can get so wrapped up in self and in trying to get ahead that we forget the importance of having and expressing gratitude. Bragging about achievement or complaining about our work fosters ungrateful thoughts, decreases our spirit, and moves us away from faithfulness. On the other hand, thankfulness yields grateful thoughts, enlarges our spirit, and increases our faithfulness to God.

We can learn to be filled with thankfulness for the wonderful opportunities—and challenges—that our work presents. We can more fully understand that work is ordained by God to reflect His glory. Our workday can be filled with joy as we wholeheartedly praise and acknowledge God for the blessing of work, which He so graciously provides.

Maybe that sounds a bit facetious. But is it really? According to Scripture, it's not really a stretch at all. In First Thessalonians 5:16-18 we are instructed: "Be joyful always; pray continually; give thanks in all circumstances, for this is God's will for you in Christ Jesus." From this viewpoint, gratitude is expressed in all we do. Our work, indeed, is a blessing from God, which provides for our needs, gives us something productive to do, and allows us to positively impact others as we carry out the purposes for which we are created.

## GRATEFUL ATTITUDES

Unfortunately, work is often overlooked when it comes to expressing our gratitude. We may give thanks for a nice day, our house, or the food we eat. But how often do we express gratitude for our work? We may not feel grateful because we feel underappreciated, overworked, or underutilized.

We may harbor resentment because no one ever thanks us for the work we do. There are a number of reasons for frustration, disappointment, and thanklessness at work. However, we need to rethink our circumstances—and our attitude. Nothing more quickly diminishes our work life than an ungrateful attitude. Conversely, nothing more quickly improves our work life than a thankful and grateful mindset. God provides work to be a blessing as well as a means to support and sustain other blessings. When our hearts and souls are filled with gratitude, our thoughts and words will reflect praise and thankfulness for all that He has done: "But giving thanks is a sacrifice that truly honors me. If you keep to my path, I will reveal to you the salvation of God" (Ps. 50:23 NLT).

---

**God provides work as a blessing.**

---

We have all encountered people who take all of the credit for their success without thanking those who helped them along the way. Often these individuals are insecure and unhappy. On the other hand, those we meet who are grateful and willing to praise others usually have a propensity to lead fulfilled and joyful lives. Business owners, leaders, and highly successful professionals always should be among the most grateful. After all, they often have much for which to be thankful and have benefited greatly from the support of others. An appreciative boss who regularly thanks God, employees, customers, and others sets a standard of gratitude for the entire organization. It is of great importance for leaders to be keenly aware of the influence that their gratitude will have on those around them.

Employees, regardless of your boss's level of gratitude, you are responsible for your own attitude of thankfulness. Do not be negatively influenced by others. Set your own tone of grateful appreciation. Consider these questions:

- When was the last time I wholeheartedly thanked God for the work He has given me?

- When was the last time I genuinely thanked my boss or supervisor for the work they have provided me?

What would your boss think if you stepped up and said, "I just want to thank you for the work you provide for me?" Sincere appreciation and heartfelt thanks go a long way. People love to hear the words *thank you*. By thanking others, you pass on your gratitude and encourage them with your uplifting attitude of sincere appreciation.

Diverting our praise to God and thanking others tends to multiply our blessings. Gratitude is an endearing quality that not only lifts our own spirits, but also lifts the spirits of those around us. Once our attitude of gratitude has reached the heart level, people will begin to see a difference. When we are grateful for our work, we find more enjoyment, fulfillment, and satisfaction in all we do.

> *So I saw that there is nothing better for people than to be happy in their work. That is why we are here . . .* (Ecclesiastes 3:22 NLT).

## GRATEFUL WORSHIP

Our work provides an opportunity to worship God. Work was mandated—and blessed—by God at creation: "The Lord God took the man and put him in the Garden of Eden to work it and take care of it" (Gen. 2:15). In this Scripture passage, the original Hebrew word translated "to work" is *a'vodah*. The word *a'vodah* actually has dual meanings. It can be translated to mean both work and worship. Therefore, work could be considered the original form of worship. Before there was a church, a song, a creed, or any other form of worship, there was a workplace: the Garden. Adam worshipped God by caring for His creation. Adam's work, indeed, was an expression of his worship. So is ours.

Far too often, we try to compartmentalize our worship by thinking worship is what we do at church on Sunday and work is what we do the rest of the week. As we more fully understand that God is praised not so much by raised hands as He is by committed hearts, our whole perspective of worship will begin to change. Worship is all about God and His glory. Rick Warren wrote, "Worship is a lifestyle of enjoying God, loving Him and giving ourselves to be used for His purposes. When you use your life for God's glory, everything you do can become an act of worship."[1]

---

**God is praised by committed hearts.**

---

In essence, worship is what work is all about. Likewise, worship is what life is all about. Worship places God in the center of our lives. Worship and work are one and the same when we commit our efforts to the glory of God. Each day provides opportunity for our work to be done in the name of Christ in gratitude to God. ". . . So let the peace that comes from Christ control your thoughts. And be grateful . . . .Whatever you say or do should be done in the name of the Lord Jesus, as you give thanks to God the Father because of Him" (Col. 3:15,17 CEV).

## GRATEFUL PRAISE

Worship may seem distant to us while we are under the stress of completing a project, dealing with an employee issue, taking care of a disgruntled customer, or facing household responsibilities. We can easily become distracted by the challenges at hand. When this occurs, a simple prayer of gratitude offered up in the midst of our busyness can help align our hearts with worship and fortify our souls. When things get really hectic, we can find great peace in taking a moment for a quick spiritual retreat right where we are. Bear in mind, we do not always have to bow down, close our eyes, or break out in song to worship Him. In fact, nobody even has to notice as we reenergize our worship by focusing on Him. A simple prayer of gratitude can lift us right where we are in the midst of tumultuous surroundings: "Jesus, You are Lord. Thank you for loving me. Thank you for living in me. Empower me through your Spirit. Praise be to God. Amen."

Through thanksgiving and praise, we reveal faithfulness in Him:

> *Enter His gates with thanksgiving and His courts with praise; give thanks to Him and praise His name. For the Lord is good and His love endures forever; His faithfulness continues through all generations* (Psalm 100:4-5).

Thank God for providing the blessing of work! Let our good works praise His name. We thank God for what He does, and we praise Him for who He is. He alone is worthy of our worship and heartfelt gratitude. We all have so much for which to be grateful.

As John Piper explains, "God is most glorified in us when we are most satisfied in Him."[2] A thankful heart tunes us into God's wonder and opens us to his blessings. Through thanksgiving and praise, we demonstrate our gratitude to God as we love Him with all of our souls.

---

**Endnotes**

1. Rick Warren, *Purpose Driven Life* (Grand Rapids, MI: Zondervan, 2002), 56.
2. John Piper, *When I Don't Desire God* (Wheaton, IL: Crossway Books, 2004), 13.

# Chapter 8

# Shine With Stewardship

## SERVE HIM

*What are mere mortals that you should think about them, human beings that you should care for them? . . . You gave them charge of everything you made, putting all things under their authority* (Psalm 8:4,6 NLT).

Upon first glance, the House Blend Café near Orlando, Florida, appears to be just another of those trendy coffee houses that seem to dot every corner these days. Once inside, though, you begin to sense a distinct difference. It is more than just the friendly staff and comfortable setting that make this place unique. The intention of this café is spelled out clearly on their menu:

> We really want you to kick up your feet and live life with us. Why we do this is even more important . . . so that we can give ourselves away for community service and restoration projects both here in Orange County and around the world. That includes feeding the homeless, funding services for women and children in need, helping restore neighborhoods, and supporting other people who have a heart to love and serve their neighbors.

With a purpose like that, even spending four bucks for a latté, could be deemed an act of good stewardship. Interestingly, the purpose of House Blend Café sounds more like one of a church than it does of a coffee shop.

Pastor Jason Dukes, of WestPoint Fellowship Church (WFC), explains:

> The Church was never intended to become a "place" full of programs to plug people into on Sunday mornings. The church is a "who" not a "what"; it is a gathering of Christ's followers working together to love and serve the culture around us. Instead of loading people up with church activities we want to equip people to go and be the church in their daily lives throughout the community.[1]

Dukes and some local business leaders formed a company called Restoration Concept, Inc. to become the relational and financial investment company for WFC. In February of 2006, the doors of a legitimate business—not a "church coffee house"—were opened to love and serve its community. House Blend Café is all about people. It is a place where anyone will feel welcome, can blend in, and encounter the "Who of the Church" in its truest form—engaging the culture around it in friendship and unity while performing community service projects. One hundred percent of the profits generated by the café are used for these purposes.

> "It's a matter of stewardship," says Dukes. "When God blesses us He intends those blessings to flow through us as we live 'sent lives' like a letter from God declaring His unconditional love and unfailing hope to those around us."[2]

## PERSPECTIVE OF STEWARDSHIP

A steward is a manager of someone else's belongings. Personally, I had always considered stewardship as strictly a monetary thing. In fact, I considered myself a pretty good steward due to my conservative financial management and consistent tithing. Funding God's work through tithing (generally considered as a percentage of our income) and giving (any freewill gift beyond a tithe) is indeed a valid display of obedience. But faithful stewardship involves much more than that.

Stewardship is an expression of how we choose to live our lives and how we spend our time. For instance, we are each given 168 hours per week. How many of those hours are lived devoted to God and to His purposes? Do we pour it all into a single hour of putting on our Sunday best, or do we shine all week in time spent with family, with neighbors, and in the workplace? Gathering for formal worship is significant for nourishing our souls. However, true stewardship is revealed through the other 167 hours of living each week.

Faithful stewardship requires a shift in our perspective of ownership. A steward understands that *all* things are God's. He owns it all, and He has entrusted us to care for His resources. We are merely stewards of the blessings that He provides. From this point of view, stewardship frees us to share from 100 percent of our blessings rather than from a small percentage of our income. Once we understand that all things belong to God, it is then that true stewardship begins. I may indeed be the majority shareholder of our organization. However, in reality, God owns it all. He is the real boss. He has entrusted time, knowledge, resources, and relationships to my care. In various ways and means, God entrusts each of us with work and resources. He calls us to honor Him with stewardship in all we do.

## PRIORITY OF STEWARDSHIP

Without proper stewardship, it is easy to get our priorities jumbled when it comes to our work. For many, the purpose of work is to make a lot of money. However, a steward realizes that a priority on personal riches leads to eventual loss, whereas a priority on God brings eternal blessings: "A faithful man will be richly blessed, but one eager to get rich will not go unpunished" (Prov. 28:20). There is nothing wrong with building wealth and making money. Many godly people are wealthy. But financial status is not what God measures. He looks deeply into our souls and measures our devotion to Him. Our priorities—where we spend our time and resources—reveal where our true devotion lies: "Where your treasure is, there your heart will be also" (Matt. 6:21).

God calls us to a loving relationship where Christ is Lord. That means that our lives belong to Him. As faithful stewards, we should allow Him to govern every penny we spend, every moment of our time, every thought that runs through our minds, every relationship we encounter, every action we take. It is all His. We are stewards of whatever God gives us. He is our priority, and He alone provides our purpose in life and in work.

> *If we live, it's to honor the Lord. And if we die, it's to honor the Lord. So whether we live or die, we belong to the Lord. Christ died and rose again for this very purpose—to be Lord both of the living and of the dead* (Romans 14:8-9 NLT).

When He is Lord, we no longer are driven by making money, impressing others, or building our own kingdoms. We simply place our priority on honoring Him. When we honor God with faithful stewardship, everything else falls into place.

## PROVISION OF STEWARDSHIP

Stewardship puts our work into proper perspective. God uses our work to meet physical needs for food, clothing, shelter, health care, education, etcetera. He can also use our work to meet the spiritual needs of those we encounter throughout the day. This can happen when we, as good stewards, rely wholly on His provision.

> *So do not worry, saying, 'What shall we eat?' or 'What shall we drink?' or 'What shall we wear?' . . . But seek first His Kingdom and His righteousness, and all these things will be given to you as well* (Matthew 6:31,33).

A few years back, the intended purpose of my work began to shift from growing my own kingdom to being used by God to grow His Kingdom. Others in our organization have experienced the same. This does not mean that we have stopped trying to run an effective and profitable business. On the contrary, it means that we have set as our priority the goal to be even better stewards of the profits that God provides. Our leaders frequently gather to pray for the company, our employees, and for God's Kingdom. We pray that God will use us for His glory and that we will be faithful stewards of the resources and relationships that He entrusts to us.

Sometimes we catch a glimpse of what God does through the stewardship of our work. For a time, we had a fun-loving group of young equipment salesmen covering the north Georgia region of our territory. They were excellent employees. However, I never really knew where their hearts were. During the downturn in sales that we experienced in early 2000, all but one of those guys left our company for jobs with greater income potential. I did not know what had become of a number of them until receiving this e-mail:

> Kris,
>
> I ran into Paul the other day and we discussed that you probably don't know what an impact working at Vermeer Southeast has had on our lives. We discussed that sales meeting when you first suggested the idea of SHINE to our sales team. The night before, many of the guys had gone out partying, and as Paul sat there with a hangover, listening to you talk about serving others and honoring God through your work, he made a commitment to be more responsible and intentional about letting his light shine before men.
>
> Because the company leadership openly promoted prayer and spiritual growth in the workplace, Paul invited Greg to pray with him and go to church with him; now Greg and his family are following Christ. The change in Paul and Greg's lives had a domino effect on the group—like Paul buying Eric's first Bible and Eric reading it in devotions with them in the mornings.

You have seen the depth in Monte as he's grown into a Christian leader in your company, in his church, and in his household. He has taken that accountability to a new level with his group: to shine.

Paul is now on fire for mission work in Haiti and has been involved in saving many lives and souls for God's kingdom. As you know, other than Monte, we have all moved on to other jobs, but we all still carry the SHINE vision with us. We all understand how we can make an eternal difference; all of our family relationships have improved dramatically, and we now openly talk about God and what he is doing in our lives.

I don't think you'll ever know until you get to Heaven how many people have been impacted by your equipment dealership. It was not that you ever preached to us or said this is the kind of employee you have to be, but you laid out what God placed on your heart; how our company's purpose was to shine for Christ before men. God took it from there, and now others are doing the same in other companies. Who will ever know how many lives will be changed because of SHINE. I just wanted to let you know how our time working with you has changed our lives.

Love ya dude,

Scott

## PURPOSE OF STEWARDSHIP

Nothing we experience in life compares to being used by God for His purposes. Personally, I had little to do with changing these men's lives. Jesus Christ did that. In fact, only God can grow His Kingdom. Yet, by the power of His Spirit, He works through us for that very purpose. There is no greater role that we could hope to fulfill than that of a faithful steward used by God for His purposes. When He shines through our souls, He is honored, His glory is reflected in us, needs are met through us, and God's Kingdom advances. Faithful stewardship allows us to become conduits through which God's bountiful blessings flow.

> *Now all glory to God, who is able, through His mighty power at work within us, to accomplish infinitely more than we might ask or think* (Ephesians 3:20 NLT).

---

## Endnotes

1. Jason Dukes, personal conversation Orlando, FL, March 2007.
2. *Ibid.*

Reflection

# My Purpose of Faithfulness

## SUMMARY

**Principle Two: Honor God**

One of the keys to shining beyond significance is to seek a purpose for our work beyond making money or meeting our own needs. My company's corporate purpose statement is "to honor God as faithful stewards of resources and relationships." When we honor God, our work reaches beyond ourselves and makes a difference in the lives of others. A soul of faithfulness is revealed by loving Him with heart, soul, mind, and strength. Although we don't expect every employee to embrace this purpose, we have found that those who do discover greater meaning and fulfillment in their labors. We believe that to honor God serves the greatest purpose of all.

**Application**

1. What is the purpose of your work?
2. If you own or manage a company, what is the purpose of your company?
3. What can you do in your work place to model these qualities?
    a. Trust
    b. Gratitude
    c. Stewardship
4. What is God's purpose for your work?

**Think about it:**

What is your purpose of faithfulness?

## CORE VALUE STATEMENT

*A soul of faithfulness obeys God's purpose.*

## Principle Three

# IMPROVE CONTINUALLY

*Enter through the narrow gate. For wide is the gate and broad is the road that leads to destruction, and many enter through it. But small is the gate and narrow the road that leads to life, and only a few find it* (Matthew 7:13-14).

## Chapter 9

# Ignite the Flame of Excellence

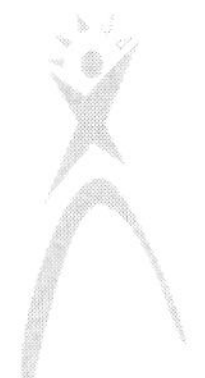

### A MIND OF EXCELLENCE PURSUES GOD'S VISION

*. . . Supplement your faith with a generous provision of moral excellence, and moral excellence with knowledge, and knowledge with self-control, and self control with patient endurance, and patient endurance with godliness*
(2 Peter 1:5-6 NLT).

At the age of twelve, I envisioned myself winning the Masters Golf Tournament. That dream drove me to excel as a golfer. By high school, my game had improved enough to receive a collegiate golf scholarship. From the beginning of my college years, many obstacles lined up to divert my attention. I progressively lost the focus and determination required to excel in competitive golf. As my vision for excellence waned, my progress in the sport halted. Eventually, I gave up on that dream.

Upon graduating from college I took a job in my dad's company. He needed employees, and I needed a job. So, it seemed like a natural fit. My role was to help out wherever needed. My unofficial title was "gopher"—go for this, go for that. My position was at the bottom of the totem pole, which was exactly where I belonged. My mind was not in it at all. Most of my time involved day-dreaming about golf and other things. I had no passion for the equipment business. It is no surprise that my performance as an employee was far from excellent.

One day, while shamelessly slacking off, I overheard some of my fellow employees talking. No one knew I was listening from the next room. They were discussing how worthless I was. They all agreed that I would never amount to anything, that all I was good for was swinging a golf club, and that the only reason I had a job in the first place was because my dad owned the company. The obstacles in my life were stacking up again.

Fortunately, this time the obstacles did not overwhelm me. Instead, they sparked a new dream. At that moment, a passion to improve myself was born within me. My new dream was to prove how much better I could be in this business than anyone else, including my dad. This newfound dream proved quite a motivator for me. Nobody would ever again point to nepotism as the reason for my employment. My motivation was admittedly off base. But it did kick-start an insatiable drive for excellence, which was fueled by continual improvement. I studied, learned, and worked hard—doing whatever it would take to move ahead. Pursuing this dream with great perseverance eventually led to a high level of personal success. However, what appeared as outwardly fulfilling a dream of excellence, ultimately felt empty inside. Eventually, I've discovered that true fulfillment is found in seeking His vision rather than in chasing my own dreams.

---

**Excellence is using God's gifts to our fullest potential.**

---

In this growing process, I have learned that anybody can dream big dreams. However, God alone can reveal *His* vision of excellence. True excellence is not found in comparing ourselves to others. It is only found in making the most of the opportunities that God affords each of us. As the focus of our pursuits shift from chasing our dreams to seeking God's vision, our capacity to grow and improve exponentially increases. God's ability to improve our lives—and our impact on life—greatly exceeds our ability to improve ourselves, as the scope of God's vision greatly exceeds our own comprehension and ability. In fact, the vision to shine with excellence is impossible to achieve on our own. It can only occur when His excellence shines in us. When Christ shines in us, we represent His Kingdom on earth. Nothing could be more excellent than that.

## AN EXCELLENT WITNESS

Excellence, the quality of being outstanding or superior, is often equated with winning a game or rising to the top of a profession. If encouraged to perform your work with excellence, you might think, "Hey, I'm not a professional athlete or the president of a company. I just do what I must to get by." You might even question whether what you do for a living really demands excellence. Do not buy into that kind of thinking, even for a moment. Regardless of your profession, God desires excellence from you.

When we give our best for His glory—no matter what that is—it is excellent. In fact, let me propose another definition for excellence. Excellence is using God's gifts to our fullest potential in carrying out the plans He has designed for us. It's doing the best we can with what we are given. Perhaps, it is being a parent or friend or doing a job well. Whatever we are called to do, excellence is an integral part of God's plan for approaching our life and our work. Because God's plans always lead to excellence, it is disconcerting when believers present less than excellent efforts in their work. I know of employers who intentionally shy away from hiring Christians because they have found many to be underperformers at work.

A friend of mine owned a large employee leasing company in the United Kingdom. He recently relayed his disappointment in the fact that many of the professing Christians he employed were some of his poorest employees, often lacking in motivation and work ethic. Knowing that he too was a Christian, they presumptuously took advantage of their boss's shared faith, viewing their jobs as entitlement, rather than as opportunity. Some, who routinely pointed out the misdeeds of others while never setting an example of excellence themselves, acted very self-righteously. This kind of report is disheartening to hear once, much less over and over.

As ambassadors for Christ, our lives at work are critical to our witness. Believers should be keenly aware that our work is under constant scrutiny by those around us. Our work should reflect the excellence of our Lord. Lazy, complaining, underperforming workers do not generate interest in the message of Christ. However, for those who soar like eagles as they serve the Lord, the influence of their work will draw positive attention as well as provide opportunities for witness to the distinctive excellence and saving grace of Jesus Christ. We are called to represent the Kingdom of God. For that reason alone, Christians should be among the top employees in any work setting.

> *Do everything without complaining and arguing, so that no one can criticize you. Live clean, innocent lives as children of God, shining like bright lights in a world full of crooked and perverse people* (Philippians 2:14-15 NLT).

## AN EXCELLENT MIND

If the quality of your work is not defined by excellence, it is time to change your thinking. Excellence begins as a thought in the mind. It is estimated that nearly 10,000 thoughts go through the human mind on any given day. All of our actions, whether good or bad, begin first in our minds as a thought. What we think about is the precursor for the actions we take. Through prayer, Scripture reading, and our pursuit of God's will, the Holy Spirit fills our minds with excellent thoughts: "Those who live according to the sinful nature have their minds set on what that nature desires; but those who live in accordance with the Spirit have their minds set on what the Spirit desires" (Rom. 8:5).

The sinful nature diverts our minds away from excellence. Prideful, negative, and selfish thoughts are all produced by the sinful nature. Contrarily, the Spirit supplies only just, godly, and excellent thoughts. What do you think about at work? Are you being led by the Spirit? Or does the sinful nature seem to control your mind? Only by the power of the Spirit can we overcome the sinful nature and rise above our negative thoughts. When the Spirit guides our thoughts, we reveal a mind of excellence:

> *The peace of God, which transcends all understanding, will guard your hearts and your minds in Christ Jesus. Finally, brothers, whatever is true, whatever is noble, whatever is right, whatever is pure, whatever is lovely, whatever is admirable—if anything is excellent or praiseworthy—think about such things* (Philippians 4:7-8).

Controlling our thoughts is paramount, because our thoughts generate our dreams. And dreams are very powerful in allowing us to think ahead, envision a desired future, and give us something toward which to aim. Dreams inspire us and stretch our vision. In business, the most successful individuals always will be those with a dream and an effective plan to achieve it. William James said, "Most people never run far enough on their first wind to find out they've got a second. Give your dreams all you've got and you'll be amazed at the energy that comes out of you."[1]

---

**Will God be glorified?**

---

## AN EXCELLENT VISION

As inspiring as possessing a dream can be, it is important to note that there is a big difference between chasing a dream and seeking God's vision. Our human minds can dream dreams. However, only God can reveal His vision. Because dreams can be so motivating, it is essential that the dreams we pursue line up with God's vision. For instance, there is a big difference between dreaming about achieving great wealth so that we can live an extravagant lifestyle versus dreaming that God will bless us financially so that we can provide for our families and help fund the advancement of His Kingdom. To be sure a dream is on the right track, ask this simple question: *If I realize this dream, will God be glorified?*

A vision of excellence always glorifies God. His vision inspires love, faith, service, and endurance. It is the vision of God's Kingdom that internally inspires and graciously lifts us to excellence beyond comprehension: "'My thoughts are nothing like your thoughts,' says the Lord. 'And my ways are far beyond anything you could imagine. For just as the heavens are higher than the earth, so my ways are higher than your ways and my thoughts higher than your thoughts'" (Isa. 55:8-9 NLT).

When our hearts and souls focus on the excellence of seeking God and his Kingdom, it is then that our mind's eye can begin to perceive the vision of His Kingdom.

---

**A mind of excellence pursues God's vision.**

---

> *. . . This is the message from the Son of God, whose eyes are bright like flames of fire, whose feet are like polished bronze: "I know all the things you do. I have seen your love, your faith, your service, and your patient endurance. And I can see your constant improvement in all these things"* (Revelation 2:18-19 NLT).

God's vision expands beyond the here and now and stretches into the ever after. God is overseeing our constant growth and using our innate capacity for improvement to prepare us for eternity. A mind of excellence continually increases *competence,* inspires *courage,* and ignites *passion* so that the excellence of God's Kingdom is clearly reflected in all that we do.

> *Then the godly will shine like the sun in their Father's Kingdom. Anyone with ears to hear should listen and understand* (Matthew 13:43 NLT).

---

**Endnote**

1. William James, www.quotationspage.com, (accessed 15 November 2007).

## Chapter 10

# Shine With Competence

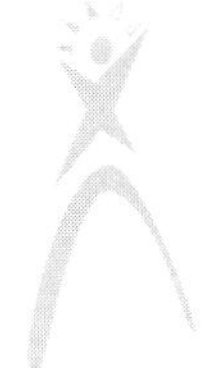

### SOAR WITH STRENGTHS

*Do you see any truly competent workers? They will serve kings rather than working for ordinary people* (Proverbs 22:29 NLT).

"Two of the most important days in your life are the day you were born and the day you discover why."

I was attending a leadership conference and these words had a powerful impact on me. The speaker that day was Kirbyjon Caldwell, pastor of Windsor Village United Methodist Church in Houston, Texas. Caldwell shared his story of growing up in a rough community, working his way out through education, graduating from the Wharton School of business, and becoming a successful Wall Street investment broker. It was evident that God had equipped Caldwell with great competence and the drive to improve continually. Each year brought more success as he continually pursued his dream. Eventually, God revealed a vision of excellence to Caldwell, which he believed clearly defined the reason for his existence: "My heart and my mind became eclipsed in what God wanted me to do."

Caldwell became consciously aware that God had gifted him with strengths and abilities that could be utilized for a much higher calling than just building personal success. Kirbyjon resigned from his high-paying position to attend seminary and ultimately take the pulpit of a small Houston church with 25 members. Today, that church has grown to over 14,000 members. But more importantly, Caldwell's vision has allowed for major impact in the surrounding community.

In a declining, deprived, and violent area of town, there is now new hope. In the early nineties, Caldwell put his business competence to work—acquiring and renovating an abandoned department store. Where there once stood a rat-infested symbol of a declining community, there now stands a 104,000 square-foot commercial center, which houses educational, health, and financial services. The development of this "power center" has played a key role in spurring economic growth, spiriting morale, and empowering holistic transformation in many lives of this community.[1] Hearing Caldwell's story that day really opened my mind to what God does through the competency of the servants He equips to seek His vision.

## DEFINE STRENGTHS

God has created each of us with unique strengths and abilities. I like to ask people what their three areas of greatest strength are. The normal response is "I don't know" or "I have never thought about that." Sometimes people are careful not to tout their strengths because they don't want to appear braggadocios or arrogant.

Here is something to consider: The reason you have strengths is because God has gifted you in those areas. When we realize that our strengths are gifts from God, we find that acknowledging and using these strengths provide opportunities to glorify Him. One of the most important things we can do for our own personal growth is to define our God-given strengths. Knowing one's strengths is crucial for any type of improvement.

Take a moment to consider and jot down the three areas of your work in which you are the strongest. (For example, mine are: leadership, communication, and coaching.)

1. ______________________________

2. ______________________________

3. ___________________________________________

Next, ask friends, family, and fellow workers to tell you what they consider to be your top three areas of giftedness. Then compare their lists to yours. These exercises can be fun and can provide you with valuable information. Once your greatest strengths are defined, you should concentrate a majority of your focus on developing and maximizing those areas. Think about ways you can improve upon the three areas of strength that you have listed.

Unwittingly we, at a young age, are conditioned not to focus on our strengths but on our weaknesses. If a child is good at reading but bad at math, teachers place the emphasis on improving the child's math aptitude. Consequently, more time is devoted to improving math skill and less to improving reading skills. This may be necessary for developing a well-rounded sphere of knowledge. However, when we get into the work force, many of us reflexively think we need to be well-rounded if we want to be successful. This is just not true. The most successful workers are those who instinctively focus their energies in the areas of their greatest giftedness.

## ACCEPT WEAKNESSES

I always ask prospective employees to tell me about their greatest weaknesses. It's amazing how uncomfortable this makes most people, especially in a job interview. Their responses tells me a lot about them. We all have weaknesses, and trying to deny them or cover them up greatly reduces our potential for self-improvement.

Early in my career, while desperately trying to prove myself, I was under the false assumption that I should be great at everything in order to get ahead. I was trying to be everything to everybody. Of course, I was not successful in doing so. I can still recall the cynical smirks when I finally admitted that I wasn't very good at very much. What to me seemed like a breakthrough of newly discovered truth was in reality just confirming what everyone else already knew: I really stink at certain things!

When we acknowledge our weaknesses to those around us, rarely is it considered new information. Admitting weaknesses does not draw attention to our flaws as much as it displays the inner strength found in self-realization. List your three greatest weaknesses at work. (Again for example, mine are: attention to detail, administration, and mechanical aptitude.)

1. ________________________________________

2. ________________________________________

3. ________________________________________

Upon listing your weaknesses, think about ways that you can work around those weaknesses rather than allowing them to hold you back.

The Bible tells us not to hide or be ashamed of our weaknesses but to acknowledge them with confidence in God's power to help us overcome anything that would hinder His working in and through us: "'My grace is all you need. My power works best in weakness.' So now I am glad to boast about my weaknesses, so that the power of Christ can work through me" (2 Cor. 12:9 NLT). God creates each of us with strengths and with weaknesses. It's part of His plan to use His strength—despite our weakness—for His glory. Acknowledging and accepting our weaknesses are necessary steps towards improving continually.

## FOCUS ON STRENGTHS

Once our strengths and weaknesses are defined, it is then important to clarify the key job responsibilities of our work (this is, what we are paid to do). By assessing our skills in relation to our job requirements, we are able to understand how well we fit our role and how we can be most effective in that position. If what you are paid to do lines up more with your weaknesses than with your strengths, it may be time to look for a different position. You will be happiest and most effective at work when your natural strengths line up with your key job responsibilities.

In our company, we have found that most positions can be narrowed down to five key areas of responsibility that lead to successful job performance. For example, the general managers of our company recently met to clarify the key responsibilities of their positions. After listing hundreds of activities, they then narrowed down their key job responsibilities to five key areas for which they are each completely accountable and responsible:

1. Providing leadership and direction.
2. Assuring profitability and growth.
3. Developing people
4. Insuring customer satisfaction.
5. Managing and procuring inventory.

Our GMs had previously defined their areas of greatest personal strength. Their next responsibility was to compare these job responsibilities to their areas of greatest competence. Based on how these lined up, they were encouraged to focus on their areas of strength and to spend a majority of their time working and improving the areas in which they are already the strongest.

## MANAGE WEAKNESSES

*In Soar with Your Strengths,* authors Donald Clifton and Paula Nelson write: "What would happen if we studied what was right with people versus what's wrong with people? Instead of focusing in on what your child or your employees don't do well, the emphasis would be on helping them do more of what they are good at and at managing their weak areas."[2]

So often we evaluate people based on what they do poorly instead of on what they do well. It is so easy to let weaknesses dominate our improvement efforts. For instance, our company's general managers are all highly qualified, top-performing employees. Each of them is unique in the strengths and abilities they bring to the team. Some are great leaders while others are great analysts. Some are strong in sales and some in operations. However, none of them are strong in all five key areas of their job responsibilities. It would be really easy to point out their deficiencies and ask them to focus on improving those weaknesses. But that is not how we are choosing to operate.

Instead, we encourage them to work with others on the team to offset their weaknesses so that they can spend more time maximizing their strengths. Based on their strengths, they all approach their job in different ways. Yet each of them accomplishes the same objectives because they delegate and work with others to shore up their weaknesses. By focusing on their strengths and managing their weaknesses, our company is able to run much more smoothly than if we expected our GMs to all do the job exactly the same way. Each of these employees works more effectively and finds greater satisfaction because they devote most of their effort to their areas of greatest competence while enlisting support in their areas of weakness. We can all grow in competence by doing what we do best and delegating the rest.

## SOAR WITH STRENGTHS

Competence is the combination of our knowledge, skills, and work habits. Top performers are never satisfied with the way things currently are. They continually seek improvement in what they do. A vision of excellence does not allow us to ever "arrive" or to know it all. No matter how much we know or achieve, there is always more to learn and areas in which to improve. The author of Proverbs wrote, "A wise man will hear and increase learning, and a man of understanding will attain wise counsel" (Prov. 1:5 NKJV). The desire to improve requires taking responsibility for growing your competence.

---

**Commitment to personal improvement always precedes corporate improvement.**

---

It astounds me how often people blame someone else for their own lack of competence. Among the excuses I most frequently hear are: "I don't get enough training," "I never get any help," and "Nobody teaches me anything." Admittedly, many companies do an insufficient job when it comes to training employees. However, this is not an acceptable excuse for a lack of competence. Each person must accept the responsibility for their own growth.

Don't sit around and wait for someone to help you improve. Take the initiative. In fact, you can take a positive step right now by listing three things that you can do in the next 30 days to improve your competence at work:

1. ______________________________

2. ______________________________

3. ______________________________

- Take responsibility.
- Learn more.
- Practice harder.
- Develop skills.
- Soar with strengths.

For a company to improve continually, the process must first begin in the mind of each employee. A commitment to personal improvement always precedes corporate improvement. If you are, or desire to be, in a leadership position, the most important thing you can do for those you aspire to lead is improve yourself. As you grow in competence—as you set the example for others to seek improvement—you become more valuable to those around you.

One of the quickest ways to grow in competence is to improve your work habits: "Never be lazy, but work hard and serve the Lord enthusiastically" (Rom. 12:11 NLT). Regardless of circumstance, we should always give our best effort to growing and improving for His glory. Increasing our knowledge, skills, and work habits leads us to reach our God-given potential. The more we grow in competence, the more we reveal His excellence.

## Endnotes

1. Jenny Staff Johnson, "The Minister of Good Success," *Christianity Today* (October 2001), 60.
2. Donald O. Clifton and Paula Nelson, *Soar with Your Strengths* (New York: Dell Publishing, 1992), 20-21.

# Chapter 11

# Shine With Courage

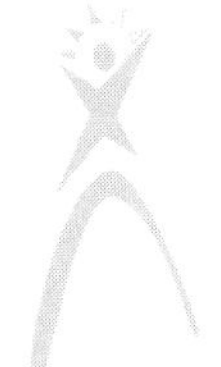

## TAKE ACTION

*Have I not commanded you? Be strong and of good courage; do not be afraid, nor be dismayed for the Lord your God is with you wherever you go*
(Joshua 1:9 NKJV).

After a couple years of college—upon giving up on my golf dream—I changed my major from business management to broadcast journalism. I promptly took an internship working for free in the sports department of a network television affiliate. This internship provided me a great opportunity to learn firsthand how sportscasters do their job as well as how they get a job. To land a job as a sportscaster, a person needs on-air experience as a sportscaster. It did not take long for me to hatch a plan.

One day, I asked a cameraman that I was helping—by carrying his equipment—if he would shoot video of me saying, "For CBS sports, this is Kris Den Besten." Next, on a Saturday night after the newscast, I talked the studio guys into staying late to tape me reading the sportscast. From these two tapings, I put together a videotape of me reporting a news story and a sportscast. I made copies of the tape and sent them to a number of smaller market television stations. Much to my surprise, I received a job offer to be the weekend sports anchor for a network affiliate television station. At the age of 20, with no formal training, no prior experience, and no college degree, I set out half way across the country to be the weekend sportscaster on live television. Admittedly, this was not very smart and lacked a bit in judgment. However, it did take a fair share of courage on my part.

Within just a few months of declaring my major I was already on the air—and frequently embarrassing myself—on live television. Needless to say, I did not become a network star. But this experience did provide a great growth opportunity and a pretty exciting part-time job while I finished my college degree requirements. After two years, I left my television career behind and retuned home with a broadcasting degree—not exactly a great educational match for the career path of a tractor salesman.

## PURSUE CHANGE

"Don't rock the boat." "Take the path of least resistance." "We have always done it this way." "It's going well now." "Why change?" "It's company policy." Do any of these statements sound familiar? They are credos of the status quo. Cried out from that dangerous pit called the comfort zone, they are the enemy of improvement—the building blocks of mediocrity.

Improving continually requires to courage to:

- Try new things.
- Step out of the comfort zone.
- Embrace change.
- Pursue a vision of excellence.

In the book *Built to Last,* a study of enduring, top companies—companies founded before 1900 and still thriving in the mid 1990s—authors Jim Collins and Jerry Porras point out the important role change plays in making a great company: "Indeed, if there is any one secret to an enduring great company, it is the ability to manage continuity and change—a discipline that must be consciously practiced, even by the most visionary of companies."[1]

The courage to change is a critical requirement for a company that desires to grow and improve. All progress requires change. It is inevitable and cannot be stopped. Proactively negotiating change is key to a successful life at work. In business, it is essential to seek positive change and to continually step beyond the comfort zone. Collins and Porras write:

> Comfort is not the objective in a visionary company. Indeed visionary companies install powerful mechanisms to create discomfort—to obliterate complacency—and thereby stimulate change and improvement before the external world demands it.[2]

## FACE FEARS

Mustering courage is mandatory as we approach any intimidating endeavor. Seeking God's vision of excellence is no different. His vision requires us to step beyond our comfort zone, rise above fear, and triumph over discouragement. It tests our faith and reveals what we believe about Him. The Bible encourages us: "Be on your guard; stand firm in the faith; be men of courage; be strong" (1 Cor. 16:13). The statements "fear not" or "don't be afraid" appear over 300 times in the Scriptures. The command to "fear God" shows up just as many times. The correlation is simple: When we fear the Lord, there is no reason to fear anything else.

> *Fear of the Lord leads to life, bringing security and protection from harm* (Proverbs 19:23 NLT ).

God is greater than all of our fears. Fear of the Lord inspires the courage to face fears and take action. Eleanor Roosevelt said, "You gain strength, courage, and confidence by every experience in which you really stop to look fear in the face."[3] Developing courage can be tough work. The good news is that if God provides the vision, He will always provide the provision to accomplish His will.

A few years ago, an industry consultant was working with our company to train employees and discuss potential changes in our management structure. I shared with the consultant the desire to use Matthew 5:16 for our company vision. He told me that, although he personally agreed with the concept, as a consultant, he could not advise building a corporate vision statement around a passage of Scripture. He warned that it could offend people and create division. He felt that we would likely lose employees and customers if we did it. He likened it to painting a big target on our company and setting ourselves up for undue scrutiny, criticism, and failure. His advice was to let God continue to guide my personal life but to keep any public reference to Him away from the business. His advice was reasonably sound, from a strictly business perspective. He had done his job as a business consultant, accentuating my primary fears of failure, criticism, and inadequacy. His advice provided an easy way out.

God, however, does not desire that we take the easy way out. He wants us to face our fears, trust in Him, and allow our work to glorify Him. We are not called to a life of comfort but to one of courage and confidence in Him. In this case, God's Word was the only business consultant we needed. It is His Word that guides us to truth and ultimate fulfillment. His Word, indeed, should frame all of our hopes, dreams, and visions. Without trusting His Word, fear would reign, and we would all miss out. I would hate to think where our company or I would be today if I had not looked ahead and relied on Him for the courage to face my fears and seek His vision.

## LOOK AHEAD

There has never been a vision-caster like Jesus Christ. His vision passes the test of time and continues to inspire infinitively. His vision of the Kingdom continually compels those who love and trust Him to look ahead to His eternal rewards: "For the Son of Man is going to come in His Father's glory with His angels, and then He will reward each person according to what he has done" (Matt. 16:27). Often, seeking His vision will require us to face challenges, forgo immediate rewards, and, by faith, look ahead. We need to take heart when the challenges are lofty and look ahead with courage. For those who seek His vision, the promise of blessing prevails.

The Beatitudes, found in the fifth chapter of the Book of Matthew, offer a brilliant framework on which to structure our thinking about having the courage to live our lives—and to conduct business—the way Christ leads:

*"Blessed are the poor in spirit, for theirs is the kingdom of Heaven"* (Matt. 5:3). Make God the boss. We must become poor in our own spirits to become rich in His Spirit. Submit to God. Look ahead, in humility, to eternal reward.

*"Blessed are those who mourn, for they will be comforted"* (Matt. 5:4). Mourn for the decadence of sin. When we confess our sins, He forgives us. Don't be defeated by sin and by personal setbacks. Display empathy and compassion. Look ahead to the blessing of comfort.

*"Blessed are the meek, for they will inherit the earth"* (Matt. 5:5). Humble yourself before God. The humble will receive God's strength and can look ahead, with confidence, to the blessing of exaltation in God's Kingdom.

*"Blessed are those who hunger and thirst for righteousness, for they will be filled"* (Matt. 5:6). Be God-centered and rely on His righteousness to consistently do the right thing. Passionately pursue God's vision. Look ahead to a life filled with blessing.

*"Blessed are the merciful, for they will be shown mercy"* (Matt. 5:7). Care for others. Be forgiving as we have been forgiven. Generously meet the needs of others. Look ahead to the blessing of being cared for ourselves.

*"Blessed are the pure in heart, for they will see God"* (Matt. 5:8). Become more Christ-like. Others will see Christ in us when we are pure in heart. Look ahead to the blessing of beholding Him face to face.

*"Blessed are the peacemakers, for they will be called sons of God"* (Matt. 5:9). Be a positive influence. Promote forgiveness over retribution. Relentlessly promote His truth and peace. Through prayer, resolve conflict and confidently face confrontations. Look ahead to the blessings that are yours as a child of God.

*"Blessed are those who are persecuted because of righteousness, for theirs is the kingdom of Heaven"* (Matt. 5:10). Regardless of circumstances, pursue God's vision. Focus beyond challenges and what others

may say about your faith. Always seek His righteousness. Look ahead to the blessing of eternal reward.

*"Blessed are you when people insult you, persecute you and falsely say all kinds of evil against you because of me. Rejoice and be glad, because great is your reward in Heaven"* (Matt. 5:11-12a). When obstacles line the path and people try to derail your witness, take courage, rise above, and with great joy, look ahead to the exciting blessings and rewards awaiting those who seek His Kingdom.

## TAKE ACTION

A while back, I was approached with the opportunity to co-host an eight week radio program to inspire listeners with the message of SHINE. My immediate response was, "Are you crazy? I don't know anything about radio. I could not possibly do that." Then my mind drifted back to those forgotten years of my past—back to a time of courage despite personal limitation. And it hit me. I have a degree in broadcast journalism. Who am I trying to fool? If I could talk about sports on television at the age of 20, I could certainly discuss God's principles for work on radio while in my 40s. Speaking to groups and recording radio programs has certainly stretched this tractor salesman well beyond my comfort zone. Yet I have found a great empowerment in Him. He always provides the courage needed for continually seeking His vision despite my doubts and uncertainties. "For I can do everything through Christ, who gives me strength" (Phil. 4:13 NLT).

Whatever we do in work and in life, His vision compels us to take action despite our fears and seeming inadequacies. Regardless of the task at hand, have the courage to give it your all, and always be open to the new path that God's vision may lead you down. The road can be rocky, and the way often narrows as we continually stumble along. Seeking His vision often will bring us to our knees. Take heart and don't forget that is right where He wants us:

- On our knees, we confirm that we cannot do it on our own.

- On our knees, the strength is found to face our fears.
- On our knees, we begin to glimpse the blessings set before us.
- On our knees, we find power to rise up and take action to pursue with great zeal the journey that is His vision of excellence.

---

## Endnotes

1. Jim Collins and Jerry Porras, *Built to Last* (New York: Harper Collins, 1994), XV.

2. *Ibid.*, 187.

3. Eleanor Roosevelt, www.quotationspage.com (accessed 15 November 2007).

# Chapter 12

# Shine With Passion

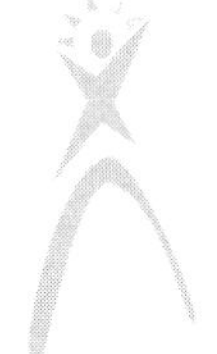

## EMPOWER YOUR POTENTIAL

*. . . I focus on this one thing: Forgetting the past and looking forward to what lies ahead, I press on to reach the end of the race and receive the heavenly prize for which God, through Christ Jesus, is calling us* (Philippians 3:13-14 NLT).

My family had just moved into the new home we built. The process had been draining, especially on my wife, and it was fraught with complications, which included three hurricanes among other countless setbacks. The stress level was high for both my wife and me. I was returning home from a particularly demanding work trip and looking forward to some down time at the new house. As I stepped through the door, my wife met me with a pointed reminder that, as the head of our household, I had the responsibility to set the level of discipline for our family. She made it quite clear that my recent performance in that role had been lacking and that the timing was perfect for me to get back on track. I was briefed on the most recent insurrections of our young children and pointed to the upstairs bedrooms where they anxiously were awaiting a meeting with me.

That evening, I sat alone and exhausted, with the weight of my responsibilities overwhelming me. Beyond parent and husband, son and friend—all priorities that I believe should come before work—I was the

CEO of a growing business, the president of our dealers association, and president of the financial board of my church. I was on advisory boards of local ministries. In the midst of it all, God had laid it on my heart to write this manuscript to share with others. With so many demanding responsibilities on my plate, I was obviously failing in my quest for a "balanced life." With my efforts seemingly sinking on all fronts, I asked God to provide a greater sense of balance in my life.

It was then that He zapped me with His omniscient truth: Balance doesn't lead to excellence. It only produces mediocrity. Balance does not inspire courage. It only promotes complacency. Balance does not spark the fuel of passion. Rather, it consumes all of our energy. We are not called to a life of balance, but one of radical imbalance—wholly and lovingly devoted to Him. He is our passion.

All of the "good things" that I was trying to do were getting in the way of my passion for Him. When we love Him with all that we are—with heart, soul, mind, and strength—the result is passion: "'No eye has seen, no ear has heard, no mind has conceived what God has prepared for those who love Him.' But God has revealed it to us by His Spirit . . . " (1 Cor. 2:9-10). That evening, God clearly revealed that I should be growing and improving my passion for Him, above all other priorities. When my relationship with Him is my top priority, His passion for excellence overflows in me and, in turn, helps energize and prioritize all the areas of responsibility in my life.

## PASSION RELEASES POWER

Above many other qualities, passion potentially is one of the most powerful. God-given passion inspires significant lives that leave a legacy. It is our passion that determines, more than anything else, where we go, how we perform, and what we accomplish. If you really want to improve in a certain area, improve your level of passion in that area. To reach for your full potential, focus on your areas of competence, have the courage to take action despite obstacles, and strive to improve continually by passionately pursuing a vision of excellence. About passion, John Maxwell wrote, "Experts spend a lot of time trying to figure out what makes people successful. They often look at people's credentials, intelligence, education, and other factors. But more than anything else, passion makes the difference."[1]

How passionate are you about life and work? Are you filled with passion, or is your tank drained? The good news is that the source of passion stands ready to fill you up any time.

> *Ask and it will be given to you; seek and you will find; knock and the door will be opened to you. For everyone who asks receives; he who seeks finds; and to him who knocks, the door will be opened* (Luke 11:9-10).

Passion is powered by these key components:

- Desire (Ask).
- Discipline (Seek).
- Determination (Knock).

## DESIRE AND DISCIPLINE FUEL PASSION

Desire drives passion. How much we want something generally determines how hard we are willing to work for it. The greater the desire, the hotter the fire of passion will burn within us. Desire creates the willpower to pursue a vision of excellence. Passionate people continually display an unyielding desire for growth and progress. Growth-oriented, passionate individuals continually seek to be better tomorrow than they are today, to be more improved next week than they were this week, and to be stronger next year than they are now. We have all been gifted with unlimited potential and the capacity for ongoing growth. Improvement is a daily process that increases over time while building on the passion of desire. We need to seek God as the driving force behind our desires and passion: "Grow in the grace and knowledge of our Lord and Savior Jesus Christ . . . " (2 Pet. 3:18). Regardless of our giftedness, we will never reach our full potential without the continual application of self-discipline. It takes boldness and discipline to pursue God's vision and to improve continually.

One of the key elements of the top-performing companies, as profiled in Jim Collins book *Good to Great,* is that each great company had created a unique culture of discipline that effectively drove the organization toward continual improvement and enduring success. Collins wrote, "A culture of discipline is not just about action. It is about getting disciplined people who engage in disciplined thought and who then take disciplined action."[2] Passion is not found in busyness and unfettered activity but in the discipline of doing a few things with passion and focused excellence. Discipline is found in seeking to do the good works, in the name of Jesus, that God has prepared for us to carry out: "For God has not given us a spirit of fear and timidity, but of power, love, and self-discipline" (2 Tim. 1:7 NLT).

## DETERMINATION FULFILLS PASSION

Determination is firmness of purpose, will, and intention. It is needed to finish a race, to complete a task, and to improve continually. A vision of excellence focused on growth will always require heroic effort and dogged determination. "Don't you realize that in a race everyone runs, but only one person gets the prize? So run to win" (1 Cor. 9:24 NLT). Determination allows us to overcome any obstacles that mark our paths. In fact, determination transforms obstacles from excuses that hold us back into motivation that inspires passion and stretches us to reach our full potential. Be determined to keep asking, seeking, knocking, and glorifying God in all you do.

Take a moment to feel the determined passion that the apostle Paul expresses in Philippians 3:13-14: *". . . I focus on this one thing: Forgetting the past and looking forward to what lies ahead, I press on to reach the end of the race and receive the heavenly prize for which God, through Christ Jesus, is calling us"* (NLT).

Paul wrote this message from jail while drawing close to his death. In spite of his current surroundings and all the accomplishments of his life's work—he chose not to look back but to look ahead to eternal glory. Paul knew he could still get better. He still hungered for growth and improvement. He continued to passionately pursue his full potential in Christ Jesus.

- Paul displayed *competence and desire* as he focused on what he did best: "I focus on this one thing" (Phil. 3:13b NLT).
- Paul modeled the *courage and discipline* to look ahead, regardless of circumstances: "Forgetting the past and looking forward to what lies ahead" (Phil. 3:13c NLT).
- Paul showed that his *passion and determination* were unwavering: "I press on to reach the end of the race and receive the heavenly prize" (Phil. 3:14a NLT).
- Paul passionately pressed on in the pursuit of God's vision of excellence: "for which God, through Christ Jesus, is calling us" (Phil. 3:14b NLT).

The passion that God provides is contagious. Like Paul, when we are filled with God's passion, it not only fills us but overflows as an inspiration for others. Passion lifts us beyond our fears and perceived lack of abilities. It allows us to climb from the pitfalls of life. Passion inspires us to do things in Him that we could not imagine doing on our own.

## PASSION EMPOWERS POTENTIAL

Without a doubt, when our works glorify God, He provides more than enough passion for us to reach our full potential. God-given passion stretches beyond our own zeal and energy, inspiring us to suffer any temporary cost that His vision may call for. Take the SHINE vision, for instance. First, God used it to inspire me to step beyond my own comfort zone. Then, He allowed it to impact our company. As it keeps our organization growing and improving, the opportunities to further this message continue to increase and take more of my time and effort.

An example is with The Jobs Partnership of Florida (TJP). This ministry focuses on decreasing poverty in the central Florida area by teaching under- and unemployed workers about God's principles for work and then placing them with local businesses in jobs that provide hope and a future. The executive director of TJP, Marc, heard of the SHINE vision from one of our employees. Marc felt the SHINE program was exactly what TJP needed to help minister to businesses in our community. The problem was, there wasn't yet a written program to use, only a few principles that God had placed on my heart to share in my own company. I honestly didn't have the time, talent, or know how to produce a training program for others. Yet, Marc wouldn't take no for an answer. When I informed him that I was not qualified to write anything beyond a sales invoice, he replied, "Kris, if you could do it on your own, then God wouldn't be needed, would He? God has given you a message. All He requires of you is your obedience and passion to pursue His will at all costs. He'll take care of the rest."

With that—despite my other responsibilities—God has fueled a passion to produce a training program, which has led to writing this book and which continually inspires me to seek His will. It certainly is not by my own intention—but by God's passion—that an equipment dealer like me is inspired and equipped to become an author. With each step in the process, God provides new and greater opportunity. Each stride requires looking ahead, facing fears, and pursuing His passion for growing, improving, and moving me ahead.

At times, we can all feel overwhelmed with work and responsibilities. Still, at other times, it is difficult to garner any enthusiasm for our work. In either case, when our passion wanes, we should stop, rest, and in stillness of spirit, mind, and body focus with heart, soul, mind, and strength on loving Him and being filled by Him. When our passion for Him is vibrant and clear, the challenges of life and work are neither mundane nor overwhelming. In Him, any work can be significant and empowering when done for His glory. God's passion releases us from the burden of our own weakness and emptiness while inspiring and energizing us with the power of His fullness. When we focus on loving Him, He lifts our potential to new levels, balances our lives as He sees fit, and lines our priorities with His. God's passion overflows with all we need.

A vision of excellence is critical for stretching to reach our full potential at work and in life. The more passionate we are, the more rewarding life and work become. God-focused passion inspires ordinary people to accomplish extraordinary things while it provides the opportunity to grow, improve, and be used by Him.

---

**Endnotes**

1. John Maxwell, *The 21 Indispensable Qualities Of A Leader* (Nashville, TN: Thomas Nelson, 1999), 83.
2. Jim Collins, *Good to Great* (New York, NY: Harper Collins, 2001), 142.

Reflection

# My Vision of Excellence

## SUMMARY

### Principle Three: Improve Continually

One of the keys to shining beyond significance is to seek a vision for our work that leads to continuous improvement. Vermeer Southeast's corporate vision statement is "to shine with excellence." Seeking a vision of excellence generates powerful momentum as our company strives to become an organization renowned for service and excellence. Even as we frequently fall short of this vision, a mind of excellence allows us to stay focused on the desired future and directs us toward the vision of what we will someday become. Excellence is revealed at the point where competence, courage, and passion intersect.

### Application

1. What are your greatest fears or obstacles that are holding back your improvement?
2. How can you overcome these obstacles?
3. What can you do in your work place to model these qualities?
    a. Competence
    b. Courage
    c. Passion
4. What is God's vision for your work?

**Think about it:**

What is your vision of excellence?

## CORE VALUE STATEMENT

*A mind of excellence seeks God's vision.*

Principle Four

# NAVIGATE BY VALUES

*Everyone who hears these words of mine and puts them into practice is like a wise man who built his house on the rock. The rain came down, and the streams rose, and the winds blew and beat against that house; yet it did not fall, because it had its foundation on the rock*
(Matthew 7:24-25).

## Chapter 13

# Ignite the Flame of Integrity

### THE STRENGTH OF INTEGRITY RISES ON GODLY VALUES

*May integrity and honesty protect me,*
*for I put my hope in You*
(Psalm 25:21 NLT).

It was lunchtime, and my kids were disappointed. If it had been Saturday or Monday or even the fourth of July, they would have been happy. But it was Sunday, and the Chick-Fil-A counter was dark and empty. My kids weren't the only ones disappointed that afternoon in the mall's food court. "I don't get it. It's just so stupid!" I heard a wife complaining to her husband. "Why would they close today? It's not like we are in the '50s anymore. Besides, they could be making so much money if they were open on Sunday."

From a typical business perspective, it's evident that Chick-Fil-A is missing out on some serious income by closing on Sundays. After all, Sunday is traditionally one of the most profitable days in the food service industry. There is, however, a pretty good reason that you will not find any of the thousand-plus Chick-Fil-A restaurants open on Sundays. Company founder Truett Cathy made this choice years ago based on his values:

> Our decision to close on Sunday was our way of honoring God and directing our attention to things more important than our business. If it took seven days to make a living

> with a restaurant, then we needed to be in some other line of work. Through the years, I have never wavered from that position.[1]

Regardless of the world's reasons for why it should be open on Sundays, Chick-Fil-A honors the integrity of its founder by living out the values on which the company is based. For Chick-Fil-A, said Cathy, "What counts in this business is not how much money we make or how much chicken we sell. What counts is the difference we make in the lives of others."[2]

## THE STRENGTH OF INTEGRITY

When your works glorify God as you serve with all of your heart, soul, mind, and strength—and Christ shines in you—others will notice. Many will be impressed. But don't get me wrong. Often people who notice will not be singing your praises. Some will call you closed-minded, irrational, or just plain stupid. Some will be angry that you won't compromise your values to benefit them. Do not be surprised by this kind of hostility. Scripture anticipates the negative reaction that may come from your choice to honor Christ: "Blessed are you when men hate you, when they exclude you and insult you and reject your name as evil, because of the Son of Man" (Luke 6:22).

If integrity was easy and always had instant positive results, more people and businesses would practice it. However, practicing integrity is not about achieving success or praise among people. It is about obeying the commands of God, recognizing His goodness, and walking in step with Him. When we focus our energy on serving others, honoring God, and improving continually, a great amount of momentum is generated. Momentum enhances performance and increases opportunities. It can make a whole company feel unstoppable. If left unguided, however, momentum can quickly take a person or company down the wrong path. Navigating by values helps channel momentum in the right direction. Values provide a guardrail, keeping momentum on the right track: the track of integrity.

Navigating by values:

- Aligns what we do with who we are, and unites our performance with our character.
- Fuses what we say with what we do, and connects our beliefs to our behaviors.

Navigating by values helps us to have integrity instead of being duplicitous. Having integrity—being who we say we are—is about genuineness and authenticity. A painting, for example, is said to have integrity if it proves to be authentically created by its named artist. A rope has integrity if it can fulfill its purpose of holding a certain amount of weight. People are said to have integrity when they practice what they preach. Still, integrity is even more than that.

Integrity is based on truth, honor, and reliability. It is wholeness, completeness, and steadfast adherence to the highest of all standards: the character of Christ. A person of integrity can be counted on at all times.

> *Those who are honest and fair, who refuse to profit by fraud, who stay far away from bribes, who refuse to listen to those who plot murder, who shut their eyes to all enticement to do wrong. These are the ones who will dwell on high . . .* (Isa. 33:15-16 NLT).

## THE VALUE OF INTEGRITY

Fearing that they can never live up to the high expectation that integrity demands, some individuals are intimidated by the idea of integrity. Yet, integrity is not perfection. In fact, there was only one person, Jesus Christ, who lived a fully righteous and perfect life. Because of Jesus, people of integrity do not have to be perfect. They simply need to believe in and follow Him. A person of integrity understands the impossibility of living a perfect life. Our imperfections are, after all, why Jesus died for us. He paid the price for our sins and our deficiencies. Because of Him, we do not need to put on a front of righteousness in order to win the approval of others. Rather, when we mess up, we can simply admit our mistakes, seek forgiveness, and move ahead in the confidence that His grace provides.

One of the clearest signs of integrity is when someone readily admits that they did something wrong. Instead of trying to hide or cover up a mistake, a person of integrity owns up. If this mistake requires repentance, a person of integrity repents. If it requires an apology, a person of integrity apologizes. A person of integrity is strong enough to overcome mistakes by confessing them before God and others. God promises to be there for those who walk with integrity: "He grants a treasure of common sense to the honest. He is a shield to those who walk with integrity" (Prov. 2:7 NLT). We all make mistakes. Yet, regardless of our past, it is never too late to seek forgiveness and, through the strength of a repentant heart, to return to the path of integrity. When we are sincere in our repentance, God promises to forgive and make us whole again.

Research indicates that the top character quality that employees desire in a boss is integrity. In a study sponsored by the American Management Association, fifteen hundred employees were asked what values, traits, or characteristics they admired in their superiors. The most frequent response was integrity.[3] Coincidently, the top characteristic that bosses are looking for in employees is also integrity. When choosing a company to do business with, people look for integrity. Based on the important role that integrity plays in the workplace, one would assume that corporate America would be beyond reproach in matters of ethics and morality. We all know how far that is from current reality.

In the competitive environment of business, an "anything goes" approach has become increasingly prevalent. The pressure to grow revenues and increase profit at all costs has taken its toll on many organizations and employees. Due to increasing incidents of accounting fraud and lack of corporate integrity, U.S. companies spent over six billion dollars in 2005 to comply with Sarbanes-Oxley financial reporting requirements, according to AMR research. These requirements have been put in place to reduce fraud in required financial reporting. According to the ethics officer association, in 1992 the total number of ethics officers in

U.S. corporations was 16; by 2005, that number had grown to over 1200.[4] Wow! Just imagine how much money could be saved and how much more effectively businesses would run if business people would simply be guided by the Word of truth and would display the integrity to walk in it.

## THE WHOLENESS OF INTEGRITY

Unfortunately, a lack of professional integrity has become far too common in today's marketplace. Many people are willing to "fudge" the truth, to "borrow" from the company, to "make small allowances" for themselves—without feeling any guilt. This comes from an attitude of "they owe it to me," rather than one of "I owe it to them." It could be so different if employees were to adapt the famous John F. Kennedy quote and let it reflect their thinking and actions at work: "Ask not what your [company] can do for you; ask what you can do for your [company]."

I recall a gentleman, who I respected for his seemingly bold faith and compassionate heart, from my church. Although I did not know him well, he appeared to be one of those people who one could admire as a pillar of integrity. I was surprised when one of his ex-employees described this man's lack of ethics at work. Over time, I heard more and more about his penchant for cutting corners, cheating customers, and treating his employees poorly. Clearly this man had been putting on a front of integrity at church while unquestionably compromising his integrity at work. Like so many others, he apparently believed that it was okay to turn on and off integrity to accommodate the situation.

It is not uncommon to find someone who claims to have integrity in their personal life yet compromises their integrity at work in order to get ahead. This is clear: If you claim to have integrity at home but not at work, you do not have integrity. There is no such thing as having a little bit of integrity. Integrity cannot be divided. It is whole and complete, or it does not exist. You either have integrity, or you don't. God does not differentiate the activities of your life. He looks at the whole. He does not apply different standards to business than He does to the rest of your life. The walk of integrity is all-inclusive.

*The integrity of the upright guides them, but the unfaithful are destroyed by their duplicity* (Proverbs 11:3).

## THE MODEL OF INTEGRITY

God sent the ideal example of integrity in His Son Jesus Christ. His life on earth provided the perfect model for true integrity. What we do (our behavior) is very important. Who we are (our character) is even more important. Most important still is who we are becoming (like Christ). Developing Christ-like character builds integrity while making us whole and complete.

I heard a story of an old farmer who took up the hobby of wood carving to pass time during his retirement. Eventually, he grew quite accomplished and his creations began drawing crowds at the county market. One of his favorite works was a life-sized eagle that he had chiseled from a large oak log. People marveled over the detail and the skill required in carving such a masterpiece. When asked how he created such a beautiful eagle from a chunk of wood, he responded, "It was easy. I just cut away everything that doesn't look like an eagle."

---

**The strength of integrity rises on godly values.**

---

This is exactly how God develops our character. He already knows what we should look like. When we yield to God and seek to personify His values, He purposefully and skillfully cuts away everything in our character that does not look like Jesus Christ. It is through this process that we are formed to become like Jesus. We are God's masterpieces. When God works in us, He shapes our character to honor and to glorify Him. We can be confident that God acts with integrity because He is faithful in keeping His promise to finish the masterpiece that our lives can be: "And I am certain that God, who began the good work within you, will continue His work until it is finally finished on the day when Christ Jesus returns" (Phil. 1:6 NLT).

As we become more like Christ, our behavior reveals the true values of our God. As we trust God and allow Him to work in us, values of integrity become evident.

- Navigating by values requires:
- *Clarity* to know what we believe.
- *Conviction* to live out those beliefs
- *Confidence* to make the right choices.

Our journey of faith is a continual process of developing Christ-like values as we become more and more like Him and as His integrity shines through us.

---

## Endnotes

1. S. Truett Cathy, *Eat Mor Chikin: Inspire More People* (Decatur, GA: Looking Glass Books, 2002), 40.
2. *Ibid.*, 168.
3. James M. Kouzes and Barry Z. Posner, *The Leadership Challenge* (San Francisco: Jossey-Bass, 1987), 16.
4. Greg Farrell and Jayne O'Donnell, "Money Section," *USA Today*, (16 November 2005).

# Chapter 14

# Shine with Clarity

## KNOW YOUR VALUES

*Now we see things imperfectly as in a cloudy mirror, but then we will see everything with perfect clarity. All that I know now is partial and incomplete, but then I will know everything completely, just as God now knows me completely*
(1 Corinthians 13:12 NLT).

In the early days, my dad and his partner set the example for our company. Their faith, entrepreneurial spirit, and strong work ethic were keys in birthing a successful equipment dealership. Their directing management style formed the parameters for how our company should operate. As the company grew, their entrepreneurial style became difficult to replicate. Employees hired in outlaying stores had limited contact with the owners and, therefore, limited guidance on how to perform. Over time, the company basically evolved into two separate organizations: the original locations and the newer stores. The flagship stores, where the owners presided, had clear direction and consistent leadership, while the outlying locations floundered with uncertainly and inconsistency.

As I took a more active role in managing the company, I had, as one of my first key responsibilities, to establish clear corporate values—which defined who we are as an organization—and to set the guidelines for how we would operate. We did not create new values. Rather, we clarified and communicated the values already existing in our company. We built on the foundation already put in place. Clarifying values helped establish the framework that would allow our company to continue to grow and improve, while maintaining the integrity of its company founders. By articulating our values, we clearly defined the financial, operational, and ethical expectations of our organization. This clarity empowered employees in our organization to carry out their individual duties while operating within the boundaries of the organization's values and ideals. In essence, the values became the true directors of the organization, and they provided the clarity to navigate through the daily challenges of work.

## SEEK CLARITY

*"I don't know."*

Right now, try saying it aloud: "I don't know." Go ahead, and say it again: "I don't know!" How does that statement make you feel? Is it hard for you say? I have found that too many people find it hard to say in public. I have observed countless employees and managers who try to fake it—sometimes even making something up instead of admitting they do not know. I believe that most people willingly accept and respect people who admit that they don't know something but are committed to finding it out. Nothing frustrates me personally more than a "know it all" pretender. Clarity is being clear about what we do and do not know. Admitting what we don't know is the first step toward finding clarity and a key to developing integrity. In fact, "I don't know" is becoming one of my most frequently used statements. Where I once thought knowing everything established an aura of importance, I have come to learn that "I don't know, but let's find out" is much more effective.

The fact is, nobody can know everything or gather all the potential available information. We live in a fast-paced world full of uncertainty. As we navigate through the challenges of life, we will continually face situations that we have never seen before. Despite the uncertainty, we will be called upon to make decisions and move ahead in certain directions. Consequently, uncertainty can cripple us if we allow it to overly delay critical decisions. Sometimes we must step out in faith and make decisions despite being unsure of the outcome. Taking clear action in the face of uncertainty is a key element for establishing leadership. Uncertainty can either be a restraint that holds us back or it can be a springboard that launches us forward.

Andy Stanley wrote, "Your capacity as a leader will be determined by how well you learn to deal with uncertainty. Regardless of the type of organization you work in, your future leadership responsibilities will be capped by your ability or inability to manage uncertainty."[1]

In the midst of uncertainty, clarity of values can become a catalyst for clear decisions. Knowing what we believe and clarifying what we value promotes confidence to navigate through the uncertainties of life and work. Above all, we must put our faith and trust in God as we seek clarity and wisdom from His Holy Spirit: "So we are always confident . . . .For we walk by faith, not by sight" (2 Cor. 5:6-7 NKJV).

## CHART YOUR COURSE

Knowing and clarifying our values is essential for living a life of integrity. Values are the core beliefs that we hold dearest and are unwilling to compromise. Clearly defined values are critical for keeping us on track as we pursue our vision. Consider it this way: If you were going somewhere you had never been before, would you just start driving and hope to eventually arrive at your destination? Of course not. Once your destination was determined, you would investigate how to get there. You would find a map, get directions, plan your trip, and monitor your progress. Living without clarified values is like driving aimlessly without direction. Navigating by values charts the course that confidently leads you forward, despite uncertainties.

I often ask people if they have ever clearly defined a goal that they would like to achieve. I have found that almost everyone has clarified at least one specific goal they would like to accomplish. However, when I ask people if they have ever clearly defined and written down a set of core values by which to live, it is a different story. Goals clarify things we would like to accomplish. Values clarify who we are. Most of us are more likely to clarify things we would like to do rather than to clarify values, which reveal who we are. Clarity is found by charting a course based on clearly defined values.

## ALIGN YOUR COMPASS

A compass points out direction with a magnetized needle that always swings to the magnetic north. The first step for setting our own compasses is defining what is most important in our lives. To navigate by values, we must first clarify our own "magnetic north" with a set of personal core values, which define the beliefs and priorities in our lives. Looking back over my life, it is amazing how often my own core values changed. Since I had never clearly defined my own values, I bounced around with no course, no clarity, and no chartable direction. Often, what I valued was whatever seemed best for me at that time. Eventually, God clarified my need to set clear personal values to mark the priorities in my life. As I prayed for God to reveal what my personal core values should be, these life priorities ultimately became clear: faith, family, integrity, and responsibility.

Having clear values helps me to stay on course and make solid choices. Any decision that comes my way can be weighed against my values before I make a choice. When I weigh my choices against my values, it helps me to find clarity. Ultimately, these values guide my decisions. Scripture says, "The man of integrity walks securely, but he who takes crooked paths will be found out" (Prov. 10:9). Let me challenge you, if you have never done so, to clearly define your own personal core values. This may take some thought and time to articulate your life priorities. If you are not ready to do so, mark this page, give it some thought, and come back to it soon. Think about what personal values best define the priorities of your life. Write them down and refer to them regularly. Align your compass.

**My Personal Core Values** (beliefs for priorities):

- ______________________________

- ________________________________________
- ________________________________________
- ________________________________________

## Set Your Sights

Just as we need clearly defined personal values to chart the course for our journey, we also need operational values to set the sights for our performance. Operational values should align with personal values to guide us in the proper direction. When operational values line up with personal values, strength of integrity is produced. The Bible instructs us: "In everything set them an example by doing what is good. In your teaching show integrity, seriousness and soundness of speech that cannot be condemned, so that those who oppose you may be ashamed because they have nothing bad to say about us" (Titus 2:7-8).

The SHINE vision provides desired goals for you to navigate toward. Within the vision are five core operational values that clarify direction and set the sights for the desired outcome: a work life that glorifies God. These five values provide clarity, focus, and alignment to the proper path:

- Servanthood
- Faithfulness
- Excellence
- Integrity
- Relationships

By lining up the compass of personal values with the sights of operational values, a clearly defined course for action is established. Clarity of values leads to a life of integrity. We must set our sights. Take a moment to define your own operational values. What values would you like to guide your performance at work? Either jot them down now or do so later.

**My Operational Values** (beliefs for performance):•

- ______________________________
- ______________________________
- ______________________________
- ______________________________

**Know Your Values**

With annual sales of around 15.5 million batteries, Interstate Batteries is the leading automotive replacement battery supplier in North America. Interstate's chairman, Norm Miller, understands the important role that clear values play in running a successful organization:

> I guess the biggest challenge as a business leader is to establish appropriate priorities; then, properly direct our efforts to maintain them . . . .Our feeling is that if we treat all of our business associates with respect, fairness, integrity, care for their needs, listen to them and professionally serve them, then we will always be building a model that will work.[2]

Clarity is essential as we approach the challenges of our work. The following questions can help define clarity in our work:

- *What does our company stand for?*
- *How does our company define success?*
- *How do I fit in?*
- *What is expected of me?*
- *How am I doing?*
- *How do I get ahead?*
- *How can I make a difference?*

Employers, help your company find clarity by providing answers to these questions for each of your employees. Make it a part of their job description, and evaluate their performance in these areas with regular communication and encouragement. If you are an employee, ask your boss to clarify these points for you. It is important for both leaders and employees to clearly understand what is expected and how well those expectations are being met. Seeking clarity and shared values promote teamwork and united direction.

All-time NFL victory leader, Don Shula—who is especially well known for coaching the Miami Dolphins to a 17-0 perfect season in 1972—wrote, "As a coach, I always carried with me a set of core beliefs, values, and convictions that supported my vision of perfection. These beliefs drove my entire philosophy of coaching. They set the context and boundaries from which players and coaches could operate."[3]

---

**Know your values.**

---

The most successful teams, companies, and individuals are those who plainly understand their core values and clearly communicate them throughout their organizations. Clearly defined values reflect:

- Who we are.
- What we believe.
- How we will live or operate.

Building our lives on godly values is much like securely following a map that leads to our desired destination. Godly values allow us to move confidently when the winds, rains, and storms of uncertainty beat upon us. The clarity of godly values sets the course for a life of integrity and directs us through all the elements of life. More important than their definition of who we are, the clarity of God's values defines *whose* we are:

> *I will bring that group through the fire and make them pure. I will refine them like silver and purify them like gold. They will call on My name, and I will answer them. I will say, 'These are My people,' and they will say, 'The Lord is our God'* (Zechariah 13:9 NLT).

---

**Endnotes**

1. Andy Stanley, *The Next Generation Leader* (Sisters, OR: Multnomah Publishers, 2003), 69.
2. Norm Miller, quoted in "Christian News," www.christianet.com (accessed 7 April 2007).
3. Don Shula, *The Little Book of Coaching* (New York, NY: Harper Collins, 2001), 11.

## Chapter 15

# Shine With Conviction

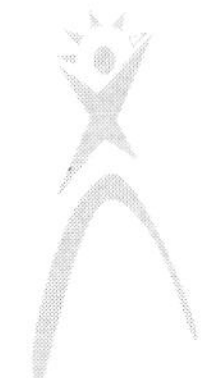

### LIVE YOUR VALUES

*For we know, brothers loved by God, that He has chosen you, because our gospel came to you not simply with words, but also with power, with the Holy Spirit and with deep conviction . . .*
(1 Thessalonians 1:4-5).

The owners of Betenbough Homes in Lubbock, Texas, share a vision to use their company's profits for promoting the Kingdom of God. This employee-owned company clearly seeks God's vision of excellence. It has established clear operational values by which to navigate:

1. Honor God.
2. Love people.
3. Be good stewards.
4. Be passionate.

With these clearly defined values marking the way, Betenbough Homes has become much more than a home building contractor. One employee described the company as "a group of people who share common goals and values united to build a home and a relationship with God."

A few years ago, that organization made a philosophical shift which took their convictions to a whole new level. Instead of being a

Christian-owned, home-building company that supports ministry, Betenbough Homes began viewing itself as a Christian ministry that sustains itself through home building. The company established a ministry department that sits atop their organization chart and is, indeed, the primary focus of their operations.

Betenbough takes their prioritized values very seriously. Exodus 23:19 teaches: "Bring the best of the first fruits of your soil to the house of the Lord your God . . . ." This company commits the first ten percent of their gross revenues to support ministries working to fulfill the Great Commission—making disciples of all the nations. That's right: The first ten percent of their gross revenue (not their gross profit) is used for ministry. In 2006, with total revenues of just over $40 million, Betenbough Homes distributed over $4 million dollars to Kingdom-building ministries. Now that's conviction!

President Rick Betenbough said, "Our priority, above even stewardship, will be to boldly strengthen our relationships—our relationship with God first, then our relationships with others, and ultimately their relationships with God."[1] How can a homebuilder from Lubbock, Texas, make such a significant impact on others? Conviction. Betenbough Homes clearly understands that navigating by God's values produces good works that glorify our Father in Heaven: "Unless the Lord builds the house, its builders labor in vain . . . " (Ps. 127:1).

## ACTION OVER WORDS

It's really not that difficult to say that we have values. Sometimes it even feels good to talk about them. In the previous chapter, we focused on the importance of clarifying values. All the work of clarifying, however, is useless if all we do is talk about values without acting on them. What we value is seen in our actions, not in our words.

> *What good is it, dear brothers and sisters, if you say you have faith but don't show it by your actions? Can that kind of faith save anyone* (James 2:14 NLT).

Navigating by values requires deep belief in and conviction about those chosen ideals. Without conviction, our values carry no influence whatsoever. Conviction enables us to live out our values.

One year, as our company compared health care benefits, my partner, who oversees insurance, met with potential providers. As the representative of a major health insurance carrier began his sales pitch, my partner noticed the company values printed on the back of this sales person's business card. At one point, my partner held up the business card and asked the sales person to expand a little on the company values. He responded, "That's just something they put on the back of our business cards. I'm not even sure what it says." Talk about a lack of conviction! It was no big surprise when—a few years later—this company experienced rough financial times due to poor service, which drove clients away.

## PERFORMANCE OVER PROMISE

It's important to note: If we are navigating by values, we have to be going somewhere. We don't navigate by sitting still. We navigate while moving ahead. As Will Rogers said, "Even if you're on the right track, you'll get run over if you just sit there."[2] We do not navigate by proclaiming values. We navigate by performing values.

These are the written core values of a famous company:

- Communication
- Respect
- Integrity
- Excellence

You would expect a company with these stated values to be a pretty good place to work at. These values could certainly lead a company to enduring success if they were lived out by an entire organization. You may not be able to guess what famous company had clarified these written core values. These are the core values of the Enron Corporation prior to its collapse and bankruptcy.[3]

It is obvious something went wrong somewhere along the way. Enron may have clarified these values, but conviction to keep them was obviously missing. These values may have been written down somewhere; however, they certainly were not being used for navigation. The collapse of Enron may have been avoided had the leadership at Enron simply followed its stated values. Many of the actions taken by some Enron employees, which led to its collapse, were completely contrary to the stated values of the company. This lack of conviction eventually led Enron to bankruptcy and cost investors nearly $60 billion in losses. Is it any surprise that a lack of personal convictions can do the same for us? If we abandon our convictions, we too can find ourselves internally bankrupt and adrift in a sea of loss and moral failure.

## CONVICTION OVER COMPROMISE

One of my favorite stories of conviction is found in Daniel 3. It's the story of three young Hebrew slaves who, due to their excellence and values, rose to prominent roles in the largest enterprise of the time. If they would just go with the flow and do as they were told, they would be set for life. As their boss, the Babylonian king, expanded his empire, he became increasingly prideful. He required all people in his kingdom to worship an idol in reverence to him. Refusal to do so led to a death sentence in a fiery furnace. The three slaves faced a crisis of belief. Outwardly, they had nothing to gain and everything to lose by defying the king's edict. However, these three were strong men of values. They knew that following their boss's order would compromise their own personal values. The three chose conviction over compromise, refusing to worship the golden idol.

The infuriated king turned up the heat higher than ever and cast the three slaves in the furnace. Things looked bleak. But then God showed up. He rescued them from the furnace. And the three emerged from the fire unscathed:

> *Then Nebuchadnezzar said, "Praise be to the God of Shadrach, Meshach and Abednego, who has sent His angel*

> *and rescued His servants! They trusted in Him and defied the king's command and were willing to give up their lives rather than serve or worship any god except their own God."... Then the king promoted Shadrach, Meshach and Abednego in the province of Babylon* (Daniel 3:28,30).

## LIVE YOUR VALUES

In today's business environment, we may not face fiery furnaces, but we will encounter countless situations that require a choice between compromise and conviction. Occasionally, compromise will appear to be the only promising option. A few years ago our company was trying to sell an expensive underground boring machine to a very large contractor. It appeared that our best shot would be to help this company complete a job by renting them our new machine. The contractor's division manager assured us that the job would be no problem and that the payoff would lead to the purchase of our equipment. Unfortunately, this particular job proved much more difficult than we were told. After a few weeks, it seemed questionable whether the job could be completed. Still we kept at it.

By week three, we had over $50,000 invested, due to the wear and tear of this difficult project. As our people began to discuss with the contractor whether we should pull out, we were informed that if the job was not completed we would receive no rental payment, no reimbursement for damage, and no possibility of selling them equipment in the future. It was clear that we were being used to complete a job that this contractor was unable to do on his own. As sales manager, it was my job to convince the company's division manager to pay for the rental and repairs of our machine, even though the job was not completed. He was very demanding and obviously under great pressure to finish this job. After debating the situation for about 20 minutes, the division manager shocked me with his next suggestion. He said that he would see to it that we got paid if I would buy him a new set of golf clubs. Talk about an easy way out of a tough situation! If I did this, we would collect all the money. And I would be viewed as a hero for doing it.

The problem was this: Doing so would compromise my core values, especially the one about integrity. "But this would be so easy," I reasoned with myself. "And was it even a compromise? This kind of thing happens all the time in business, right?" Internally, I struggled with this dilemma for a few seconds before my values made the decision for me. I told him that I knew in my heart that it would not be right. I asked him to approve the payment, regardless. As much as his request had surprised me, his answer surprised me even more. He said he would approve the payment, continue renting, and take responsibility for all of the damage to the equipment. We wound up doing a lot of business with this company over the years. I have often wondered what would have happened if had I compromised my values and given in to his request for the golf clubs.

Often making the right choice does not turn out like this did. Sometimes making the right choice can be very costly.

*What if God hadn't spared the three slaves from the fire?*

*Would my story be different if we had lost the money?*

I'm glad it worked out. But the choice still would have been right, even if the situation had turned out differently. Navigating by values is about choosing to live by values, even when it seems most difficult. Scripture tells us: "Fire tests the purity of silver and gold, but the Lord tests the heart" (Prov. 17:3 NLT). Sometimes the choice between conviction and compromise doesn't have a dollar sign tied to it. Often no one else would even know if we choose compromise. Any time we compromise our values, it comes at a great cost. You cannot put a price tag on your own integrity.

---

## Endnotes

1. Betenbough Homes, from company brochure and personal conversations 2007.

2. Will Rogers, www.quotationspage.com (accessed 15 November, 2007).

3. Carolyn B. Thompson and James W. Ware, *The Leadership Genius of George W. Bush,* (Hoboken, NJ: John Wiley and Sons, 2003), 18.

# Chapter 16

# Shine With Confidence

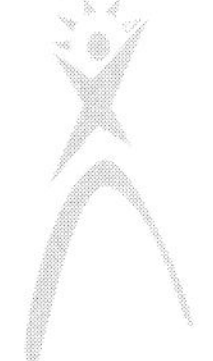

## TRUST YOUR VALUES

*Blessed is the man who trusts in the Lord, whose confidence is in Him. He will be like a tree planted by the water that sends out its roots by the stream. It does not fear when heat comes; its leaves are always green. It has no worries in a year of drought and never fails to bear fruit*
(Jeremiah 17:7-8).

We were experiencing the most turbulent decline that our industry had ever faced. Our dealership had lost over half of its revenues in a short period of time. Other similar companies were either going out of business or resorting to sweeping employee layoffs and facility shutdowns to stay afloat. Nearly a third of our fellow dealers went out of business. The financial outlook was bleak, with a forecast of extended months of famine in our industry. As business spiraled toward an indefinite bottom, an indistinguishable truth became clear: "In the fear of the Lord *there is* strong confidence, and His children will have a place of refuge. The fear of the Lord *is* a fountain of life, to turn *one* away from the snares of death" (Prov. 14:26-27 NKJV). If we were to survive this turmoil, we would need to shift our focus from the worries of this drought and trust in godly values to carry us through. Despite the economic chaos, our values steadied us with the confidence needed to weather this storm.

The following is a memo I sent our employees in the midst of the downturn:

> December 13, 2002
>
> As the year comes to a close, we want to thank each of you for your efforts and dedication to our company. 2002 has been an extremely challenging year in our industry.
>
> Due to your efforts and our vision to shine with excellence, we remain steadfast. Although our sales volume is still declining compared to last year, we still received numerous top performance awards from our factory as well as the highest achievement level in their "mark of excellence" program.
>
> Although the year is not yet over, it appears we may finish with a very small profit for 2002. In these economic times, the ability to remain profitable is quite an accomplishment. Although we are real close to the break even point, you will find enclosed a Christmas bonus. It may be smaller than in years past, but in times when thousands of companies are facing layoffs and bankruptcies, we consider ourselves extremely blessed to be able to pay a Christmas bonus to our employees.
>
> As we enter 2003, we remain wholly committed to our values and fully focused on our vision to shine with excellence:
>
> - Serve others.
> - Honor God.
> - Improve continually.
> - Navigate by values.
> - Excel in relationships.
>
> I believe if we continue to seek these things, everything else will take care of itself. We want to wish you

and your families a Merry Christmas as we look forward to a new year of challenge, opportunity, and service.

Sincerely,
Kris Den Besten
CEO

As time passed, our values provided a sense of security that motivated our employees, despite the circumstances. The values also clarified who belonged on our team and who did not. Those who bought into the values and vision of our company found peace and confidence that our values would carry us through. Those who did not buy in were freed to seek their own values elsewhere. Thanks to the stabilizing effect of our values, we survived this tough time without a single employee layoff and without shutting down any of our stores. Our values and vision worked together, defining our direction and setting our course while growing our confidence by strengthening our team.

## SET THE STANDARD

When our company first rolled out our corporate values years ago, it wasn't pretty. Some really unsettling issues began to surface in our organization. Employees who had witnessed questionable behavior in the past without reporting it found new confidence to call out activities contradictory to our newly-stated values. In one instance, we discovered that a salesperson had been selling equipment at very low prices to a company competing with some of our customers with which he was secretly a partner. We also found employees selling items for cash, pocketing the proceeds, and writing off the inventory as lost. Other inappropriate activities, which were previously unknown, began to be revealed. Initially, learning of these improprieties was extremely disheartening. Yet, in time, we understood that it was just our values filtering out the beliefs and behaviors that did not belong in our organization. Our values set the standard which clearly defined our company's expectations.

Eventually the aforementioned economic downturn bottomed, and our sales revenues began to climb. A dramatic downturn like this often provides great opportunity for those who weather the storm and cling to the strength of their values. As business picked back up, our company was able to make a number of acquisitions at the right time and the right price which have helped to strengthen our organization and accelerate our growth. In essence, our values steadied us in tough times, filtered out unacceptable behavior, and fortified our confidence for upcoming expansion.

## LAY THE FOUNDATION

As our company grows, we find that our values and vision attract like-minded individuals who share our ideals and want to join our team. As we continue to expand and acquire more territory, it is our values and vision that bring us the right people for sustaining our growth. I have discovered that the best source of employee recruitment is found in establishing godly values, and then praying that the Lord will provide the right people to live out the values and seek the vision. When we build our team on godly values, we establish a firm foundation. Jesus said,

> *Anyone who listens to My teaching and obeys it is wise, like a person who builds a house on solid rock. Though the rain comes in torrents and the floodwaters rise and the winds beat against that house, it won't collapse because it is built on bedrock* (Matthew 7:24 NLT).

Our company has experienced some great growth over the past few years. We have more than doubled the size of our territory, we have almost tripled our sales revenues, and we have greatly expanded our team of employees. As important as our values proved to be during the storms of turmoil, they are equally, if not more, important as we experience continued growth and success. Without staying firmly grounded in Christ-like values, the trappings of success could divert us from our vision. Worldly values—like wealth, pride, and power—could pull us off course and direct us toward selfishness, rather than godliness. Regardless of what is going on around us, values establish a solid foundation of character that cannot be shaken. It is from this foundation that our confidence rises, allowing us to stand firm in our values, despite any circumstance, good or bad.

## SECURE STABILITY

Life generally comes at us at a very fast pace. Every day we face new challenges at work and in life. Adversity, temptation, and uncertainty lie in wait around every corner. Moral and ethical choices mark the roadways of our journey. In business, the winds of change continually are blowing. For a business to endure, it must find its way through the peaks and valleys of time. The founder of Wal-Mart, Sam Walton, once said, "You can't just keep doing what works one time, because everything around you is always changing. To succeed you have to stay out in front of that change."[1]

- Strategies change.
- Markets change.
- Organizational structures change.
- Employees change.
- Managements change.
- Goals and objectives change.
- Compensation programs change.
- Customers change.
- Products change.

Change is constant. It brings discomfort. However, with change comes great opportunity. With everything changing all around us, great confidence can be found in core values that never change. A company grounded in values finds the confidence to allow change to strengthen and improve the organization.

An employee or owner who navigates by personal and operational values holds a distinct advantage in coping with change. Navigating by values instills the attitude of confidence. Trusting in godly values develops godly character which results in greater integrity. Integrity builds the confidence that we need to navigate through the storms of change and to come out shining brighter and stronger on the other side.

## TRUST YOUR VALUES

Confidence is founded in our beliefs and behaviors. Both belief and behavior are critical elements of life; however, they do not automatically reflect each other. Integrity happens when our beliefs, behaviors, and actions all line up. It is our belief in Jesus that sets the course for our life's journey. Accepting the salvation of Christ makes Heaven our eternal destination. Yet, it is our behavior and witness that allow us to represent His Kingdom on the earth. Think about it: Does your life represent His Kingdom? Do your beliefs and behaviors line up with godly values? When our beliefs and behaviors are firmly rooted in Christ-like values, we can stand firm in the confidence that leads to our destiny. As Rick Warren said,

> "Jesus did not die on the cross just so we could live comfortable, well-adjusted lives. His purpose is far deeper: He wants to make us like himself before he takes us to heaven. This is our greatest privilege, our immediate responsibility, and our ultimate destiny."[2]

One thing very clear is that we cannot reach our destiny of becoming like Christ on our own. We need the Holy Spirit living in us and revealing His values through us. Just as a tree does not immediately produce fruit, neither do we immediately affect the world. A tree needs time to go through the process of becoming a fruit-bearer. The proper elements must be in place for a tree to produce good fruit. Fruit is the product of what takes place in the growth of the tree. Likewise, as we grow in the Lord, His Spirit works in us, bringing the proper elements together so that we can bear good fruit: "The Holy Spirit produces this kind of fruit in our lives: love, joy, peace, patience, kindness, goodness, faithfulness, gentleness, and self-control . . . " (Gal. 5:22-23 NLT).

Over time God uses the circumstances of our lives to develop our character. The power of His Spirit enables us to do what we cannot do alone: Bear good fruit that reveals His character. Christ-like character is only revealed by yielding to Him and allowing His Spirit to work in us to produce His fruit.

So where—or in whom—should you place your confidence?

- Place your confidence in wealth, and you will be left empty.
- Place your confidence in power, and you will be left alone.
- Place your confidence in others, and you will be disappointed.
- Place your confidence in yourself, and you will be confused.
- Place your confidence in your feelings, and you will be wrong.
- Place your confidence in God's truth, and you will be secure.

Therefore, set the standard, lay the foundation, and secure stability. Place your confidence in God's values, and you will shine.

---

## Endnotes

1. Sam Walton, *Made in America*, (New York: Doubleday, 1992), 249.

2. Rick Warren, *Purpose Driven Life*, (Grand Rapids, MI: Zondervan, 2002), 178.

Reflection

# My Values of Integrity

## SUMMARY

### Principle Four: Navigate by Values

One of the keys to shining beyond significance is to navigate by clearly defined values. In the 1990s, we rolled out these corporate values to our company as an extension of our founders' business beliefs. These values and actions set the course for our corporate beliefs and behaviors as our company grew larger and expanded. It was in 2001 that God revealed the SHINE vision, which lines up with the guidance that these values have provided for so many years to our company. Our corporate values are:

- **Servant Leadership:** We will provide service and support that empowers others to reach their full potential.
- **Honesty:** We will be truthful, do the right thing, and treat people with respect.
- **Dependability:** We will build trusting relationships through quality, performance, and consistent effort.
- **Caring:** Realizing we can't always please everybody, we will seek to be understanding, supportive, and thankful for our opportunities.
- **Profitable:** We will use our profits to grow and improve, to provide for needs, and to positively impact our community.

- **Teamwork:** By uniting skills and efforts around common goals, we accomplish more together than we would alone.

The SHINE vision clarifies and expands on these corporate beliefs, behaviors, and actions. When we seek the SHINE vision, we navigate by these values, which set our course, make our decisions, and propel us ahead with the strength of integrity.

### Application

1. What values do you want to be remembered for living out?
2. How could clear values help you make clear decisions?
3. What can you do in your work place to model these qualities?
    a. Clarity
    b. Conviction
    c. Confidence

### Think about it:

What are your values of integrity?

## CORE VALUE STATEMENT

***The strength of integrity rises on godly values.***

## Principle Five

# EXCEL IN RELATIONSHIPS

*A new command I give you: Love one another.*
*As I have loved you, so you must love one another.*
*By this all men will know that you are My disciples,*
*if you love one another*
(John 13:34-35).

## Chapter 17

# Ignite the Flame of Relationships

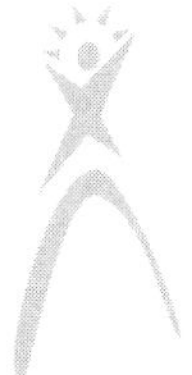

### LOYAL RELATIONSHIPS FLOW FROM GOD'S LOVE

*. . . Love your neighbor as yourself*
(Matthew 22:39).

Early in my sales career, I was only about getting sales. Whatever it took to close the deal is what I aspired to do. I set lofty goals, and I almost always exceeded them. The big picture did not exist for me—only getting the sale and moving on to the next deal mattered. Every activity was to promote my own personal agenda. The needs of others did not concern me. I just wanted to sell something and move on. If I could not sell something, I would always ask for a referral. Who could be next on my list of potential "victims"? Selling was something I did to people, not something I did for them. Building relationships was the furthest thing from my mind. This aggressive approach brought me a lot of sales success but no sense of significance. It was just business.

Thankfully, God progressively took hold of my work life and revealed an important truth to me. The way I was working would not attract people to His Kingdom. It would only build my own. We are not given work strictly for our own benefit. Rather, our work is given as an opportunity to shine His light and draw others to His Kingdom. When it is all said and done, nobody will care about how much we sell or how successful we become. It will be the relationships that we build along the way that will truly make a difference.

A life is not significant unless it positively affects the life of someone else. Our work should focus on making a friend before making a sale and on making a difference before making a profit. " . . . Pursue righteousness, faith, love and peace, along with those who call on the Lord out of a pure heart" (2 Tim. 2:22). It's not just business. It is about building relationships, making a difference, bringing value, and positively impacting the lives of others. Understanding, respecting, and appreciating others builds loyal relationships.

---

**Our work should focus on making a friend . . . not just a profit.**

---

Incidentally, establishing loyal relationships not only makes a difference, it is also much more profitable than earning a quick buck. When we build loyal relationships, we are not only rewarded today, but we establish long-term opportunity as well. Long-term relationships are always worth more than any one-time sale. Sales bring revenues today, but relationships extend far into the future.

This section, "Principle Five: Excel in Relationships," focuses on relationships, and it is slightly different than the other sections. The first four sections of the book are action-driven whereas this section deals with the result of those actions. When we serve others, honor God, improve continually, and navigate by values, the result is that we will excel in relationships. Loyal relationships are the product of living out the first four principles of SHINE. We shine when we reveal a heart of servanthood, a soul of faithfulness, a mind of excellence, and strength of integrity. When our actions reveal these values, we build loyal relationships and find great pleasure and reward in our work.

> *Moreover, when God gives any man wealth and possessions, and enables him to enjoy them, to accept his lot and be happy in his work—this is a gift of God* (Ecclesiastes 5:19).

## REFERRALS VS. RECOMMENDATIONS

Referrals are highly coveted in the business world. They provide the quickest, easiest, most inexpensive way of finding future opportunity. Referrals are valuable because they help develop more business. Personally, I do not care much for referrals. I would much prefer a recommendation. You see, a referral falls short of a recommendation because of one important aspect that is missing: relationship. The difference between a referral and a recommendation is a relationship. You may refer someone you have heard about. However, you will only recommend someone you have a relationship with. A recommendation is much stronger than a referral because it is personal. It goes beyond a suggestion, and it becomes an endorsement based on a favorable experience and relationship. For example, note the difference between the referral, "If you need a brush chipper, there is a place down the road that sells them," and the recommendation, "If you need a brush chipper, go to Vermeer Southeast. I know them, and they will take good care of you."

Referrals can happen by chance, but recommendations are always earned. We can ask a stranger for a referral. A recommendation, however, can only come from someone who knows us. In business, few things are as valuable as a recommendation. We can spend big dollars on advertising, promotions, and training. Yet, if we are unable to build relationships that earn recommendations, our future will not be secure. That is why my company's mission statement strategically includes "to earn recommendations by serving with integrity." Recommendations are critical to the ongoing success of any enterprise.

As an employee, what greater compliment could you receive than a recommendation? I know what you're thinking: *More money would be a pretty nice compliment. Wouldn't it?* The problem is, far too many employees set their focus on wanting more money, instead of on doing what it takes to earn a recommendation. Think about it. What usually comes first—a recommendation or a sale, a recommendation or a promotion, a recommendation or a raise? When we earn recommendations, good things follow. And, because we have earned those good things, we can enjoy them even more. We shine when, rather than just seeking referrals, we focus on building loyal relationships that earn recommendations. A focus on meeting needs, working together, and valuing each other builds loyal relationships that can last a lifetime.

## GREAT DEAL VS. GREAT RELATIONSHIP

In the business world, we often encounter stiff competition. Our competitors may have a better price, better marketing, and perhaps, a better product. However, they can never take away the relationships that we build with others. A loyal relationship is worth more than any other feature, advantage, or benefit.

Often, when we lose a deal to one of our competitors, we will try to blame the price or the product as the reason that we did not get the deal. Often we are too quick to look for excuses. In most cases, the true difference-maker is the strength of relationship between supplier and customer. Far too often we focus on product, price, or procedure when we really should focus on people. When we center our attention on revenues and profits, it rarely leads to relationships. However, a focus on people and relationships typically leads to increasing revenues and continuing profits.

---

**Focus on people rather than product, price, or procedure.**

---

Often employees change jobs to make more money somewhere else. We once had a talented young employee leave our organization for a better offer in a different industry. We were shocked and disappointed that this particular individual would leave our company for just a few more dollars somewhere else. Eventually, we learned that the real reason this employee left was due to a strained relationship with his immediate supervisor. He left because he did not feel that his potential or his contributions were valued by his boss.

In reality, the main reason that most employees leave an organization is not because of dollars but because of relationships. I have heard it said that over 70 percent of employees who change jobs do so because they do not feel valued by the company they left. When relationships are strong:

- The employee feels valued.
- The employee's work is more rewarding.
- The employee's job satisfaction soars.

Always remember that relationships are a two-way street of give and take. Whether you are an employer or an employee, you are responsible to hold up your end of the relationship. Each of us—regardless of our position—should take the lead in building relationships of trust. As John Maxwell says, "People respect a leader who keeps their interests in mind. If your focus is on what you can put into people rather than what you can get out of them, they'll love and respect you—and these create a great foundation for building relationships."[1]

Loyal relationships promote teamwork, interdependence, and strength. Relationships allow us to work through any situation that may arise. We are all fortified in the synergies of our relationships:

> *Two are better than one, because they have a good return for their work: If one falls down, his friend can help him up. But pity the man who falls and has no one to help him up* (Ecclesiastes 4:9-10).

## RELIGION VS. RELATIONSHIP

People enjoy their work more when they have strong relationships with their coworkers. That's how God made us. He created us to enjoy relationships with one another. He designed us to build relationships that last a lifetime and continue into eternity. Indeed, the major difference between Christianity and other religions is that Christianity is not about religion. It is about relationship. We are created for a relationship with God. In fact, it is only through a personal relationship with Jesus Christ that we find out what life is really all about. It is through this relationship that we are empowered by the Holy Spirit to do good works that glorify our Father in Heaven. It is this loving relationship with Christ that we are called to share with others. And we don't just refer others to Christ because we have heard of Him. We recommend Him to others because we know Him, because we trust Him, because we count on Him, and because we enjoy a loving relationship with Him.

## THE GREAT COMMISSION REVEALS SHINE

When the Light of Christ shines in us, others will be drawn to that light. We should always be prepared to explain the source of this light to others. We shine when our relationship with Christ is clearly seen and felt by those around us. Jesus called all believers to share this relationship with others.

> *Therefore, go and make disciples of all the nations, baptizing them in the name of the Father and the Son and the Holy Spirit. Teach these new disciples to obey all the commands I have given you. And be sure of this: I am with you always, even to the end of the age* (Matthew 28:19-20 NLT).

Note that all aspects of the Great Commission revolve around ongoing relationships. The Great Commission calls us to build loyal relationships with others, bring them to relationship with God, grow together in discipleship, and walk together in fellowship and obedience—all of which flow from the loving relationship of our God living in us.

> **S–Serve others.** "Go and make disciples of all the nations . . . " (Matt. 28:19a).
>
> **H–Honor God**. " . . . Baptizing them in the name of the Father and the Son and the Holy Spirit" (Matt. 28:19b).
>
> **I–Improve continually.** "Teach these new disciples . . . " (Matt. 28:20a).

**N–Navigate by values.** " . . . to obey all the commands I have given you" (Matt. 28: 20b).

**E–Excel in relationships**. "And be sure of this: I am with you always, even to the end of the age" (Matt. 28:20c).

The most effective way to share our relationship in Christ is by building relationships with others. Loyal relationships are built on positive responses to the following questions:

- *Can I trust you?* (Credibility)
- *Can I count on you?* (Perseverance)
- *Do you care about me?* (Love)

The answers to these questions reveal a lot about a person. From a work viewpoint, employees who can be trusted, who can be counted on to perform with excellence, and who care about others will always earn recommendations. Better still, when our lives reveal credibility, perseverance, and love, we excel in relationships that can make an eternal impact. My pastor frequently mentions that there are only three things that we can take with us to Heaven: our faith, our family, and our friends. It stands to reason that we should live focused in these three areas, growing relationships that represent, reflect, and recommend God's Kingdom both now and for eternity.

---

## Endnote

1. Maxwell, *The 21 Indispensable Qualities of A Leader*, (Nashville, TN: Thomas Nelson, 1999), 108.

# Chapter 18

# Shine With Credibility

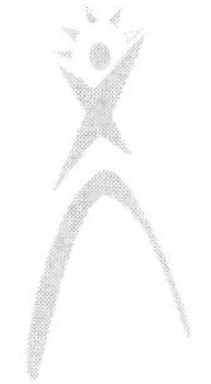

## CAN I TRUST YOU?

*Do your best to present yourself to God as one approved,*
*a workman who does not need to be ashamed and*
*who correctly handles the word of truth*
(2 Timothy 2:15).

I recently shared my testimony in what many consider to be the toughest environment in which to do so: a roomful of my peers. I was addressing this group as I wrapped up a two-year term of serving as the president of our dealers association. The room was filled with fellow equipment dealers, business managers, factory executives, key vendors, and their spouses for the banquet at our annual meeting. As the program drew to a close, the time came for me to pass the gavel to the incoming president. As I did so, I took an extended and somewhat awkward pause. A hush came over the room as I, contemplating my next move, stood silently.

Some of these people had known me for my whole career. They had known the cocky young kid who cared only about playing golf and having a good time. They would surely remember the insecure attention-craver who had often gone too far trying to prove his worthiness. Yet, others only knew me as the confident leader who had given his best to serve the association for the last few years. The safe move would be to introduce the new president and quietly take my seat.

Suddenly the words, "Before I sit down, I have one more thing to share with you," came out of my mouth. There was no turning back now since every eye in the room focused in on me. "A few years ago, I realized how messed up I was. I was living one life at work, another life at home, and still another at church on the weekend. Then, in one of those defining moments, spent alone with my creator, God revealed a profound truth. I have only been given one life to live, and I need to live it consistently with a new vision, a vision for a life wholly committed to honoring God in all I do," I said.

I went on to explain how vision allows us to be motivated by who we could become rather than being held back by our past or current situations. I progressively walked them through the principles and values of the SHINE vision as I encouraged them to seek the same. Finally, I passed the gavel to our new president. After a few very nice words from him—regarding my leadership—I sat down.

I noticed tears in my wife's eyes as she mouthed the words, "I am proud of you." Looking up, I was surprised to see the entire audience on their feet and applauding. It was at that moment that I fully understood the true meaning of the SHINE vision. Whether the crowd understood it or not, their applause was clearly not for me. Their praise and appreciation was not given for any good work of mine but for the glory of my Father in Heaven. He had given me the credibility to shine.

> *Let your light so shine before men, that they may see your good works and glorify your Father in Heaven* (Matthew 5:16 NKJV).

## DO WHAT YOU SAY

The first mark of credibility is established when we live up to our promises. It is revealed when our actions match our words. It is found in doing what we say we will do. Credibility rises on the firm foundation of honesty. Personal resumes, for example, can lack credibility. Employers, how often have you looked back at someone's resume and wished that the employee would live up to what it says? Often on a resume or in job interview, people try to make themselves look better than they really are. When this is the case, the entire employment process begins with a lack of credibility. It's doomed before it even gets started.

Employees (or job-seekers), let me encourage you to closely read over your latest resume. Does it adequately describe who you are and what you do? Or is it designed to make you look better than what your track record proves? If it's the latter, you have a choice. You can change your resume and lower it to your actual performance, or you can improve your performance and start doing what your resume says you will do. That's credibility.

Employers, do you provide everything that you have promised to your employees? How about to your customers? Does your business seek to live up to its hype?

Credibility is dong what you say you will do, and it is living up to who you say you are. Scripture exhorts us: "... Be an example to all believers in what you say, in the way you live, in your love, your faith, and your purity" (1 Tim. 4:12 NLT).

## DO WHAT YOU SHOULD

Credibility takes time. It is developed through a lasting track record of success. Credible employers pay their bills on time and live up to every obligation. Credible workers get things done. They do not make excuses but always come through by meeting or exceeding expectations. They are prompt, they meet deadlines, and they can be counted on at all times. They do not take shortcuts or skimp on quality. They do not grumble and complain. Rather, they display an eagerness to model Christ with positive words and actions. They don't bow to emotions or make decisions based on popularity.

> *Obviously, I'm not trying to win the approval of people, but of God. If pleasing people were my goal, I would not be Christ's servant* (Galatians 1:10 NLT).

Credible decisions are based on choosing what is right over what is popular. Credibility is standing for beliefs and ideals in all circumstances by choosing God's way, especially when the pressure is on. Serving Christ by working for Him may not always be popular, but it is always right. At work, Christians reveal credibility when their work reflects a witness for Jesus Christ. Charles Swindoll says:

> The very best platform upon which we may build a case for Christianity at work rests on six massive pillars: integrity, faithfulness, punctuality, quality workmanship, a pleasant attitude, and enthusiasm. Hire such a person and it will be only a matter of time before business will improve . . . people will be impressed . . . and Christianity will begin to seem important.[1]

Credibility is clearly found in God's Word. Adhering to it yields a bountiful return: "And the seeds that fell on the good soil represent honest, good-hearted people who hear God's word, cling to it, and patiently produce a huge harvest" (Luke 8:15 NLT). The seed is always good because it is the Word of truth, and it carries unlimited potential. Only the soil, in which it germinates, differs. The soil of our character determines the harvest that we produce. Through the credibility of God's Word, we produce a crop beyond our wildest dreams—a crop that produces good works that glorify our Father in Heaven.

## DO IT WELL

Credibility is also built when you do your job well. The more knowledgeable you become in your field of endeavor, the more credible you become.

- Strive to become an expert who knows your work well.
- Strive to become the type of person others seek out for answers to their questions.
- Strive to become someone who always performs with excellence.

- Strive to become an encourager who always focuses on relationships.

Striving in these ways will help you to develop great credibility while earning the recommendations of those you work or come into contact with. Usually, we think the most valuable business recommendations come from customers. A recommendation, however, can come from anyone with whom a positive relationship has been established.

Many years ago, our company purchased a pressure cleaning system from a specific vendor. Over the years, we have also purchased other items from this supplier. On a recent visit, a representative of this vendor asked if we had sold a new machine to a particular customer. It turned out that we had. This pleased the salesperson who gladly revealed that he had recently recommended our company to this customer. He explained that for years he has admired how our company does business. His experience has been one where we have always lived up to everything that we said we would do—paying our bills on time, treating him with respect, and always working together to resolve all issues. He also stated that years ago one of our competitors also purchased some equipment from him; however, that relationship had turned out much different.

Our competitor had often been confrontational, verbally abusive, and late on paying their bills. Over time, our credibility with this vendor has fostered a favorable relationship. The salesperson went on to explain that, because of this relationship, he has been recommending our company for over 20 years to every customer he knows in our industry. Who knows how many sales can be attributed to the recommendations of this supplier? Because of credibility, he trusts us enough to tell others about our relationship.

## SHINE REVEALS CREDIBILITY

Credibility draws the attention of others. People respect, listen to, and trust those who have proven their credibility. Loyal relationships are founded on the strength of credibility. When Christ shines in us credibility is a result.

**S–Serve others.** A heart of servanthood glorifies God by helping others. *Humility* is putting others first. If we care only about ourselves and our own agenda, others know it. By letting go of our ego and perceived rights, we are able to pick up joy and strength to foster credibility. One of the quickest ways to lose credibility is through a selfish attitude. Conversely, when our motives are focused on others rather than on ourselves, we gain credibility. Build credibility by serving others.

**H–Honor God.** A soul of faithfulness obeys God's purpose. *Trust* is depending on Him. By trusting in God, obeying His Word, and leaving our outcomes to Him, we earn the trust of those around us. A focus on following God's will and faithfully pursuing His purpose provides motivation, direction, and strong credibility. Build credibility by honoring God.

**I–Improve continually.** A mind of excellence pursues God's vision. *Competence* is soaring with our strengths. A lack of competence leads to poor performance and excuse-making, which destroys credibility. By soaring with our strengths and managing our weaknesses, our competence grows, allowing us to conquer complacency and rise above the status quo. When we pursue God's vision, we grow toward becoming all that God created us to be. Competence breeds credibility. Build credibility by improving continually.

**N–Navigate by values.** The strength of integrity rises on godly values. *Clarity* is found in knowing our values. Without clearly defined values, it is easy to get off track. A lack of values leads to compromise, a lack of confidence, and a decline in credibility. Clear values help us to make clear decisions personally, professionally, and corporately. Values of integrity keep us on the right track and reveal credibility. Build credibility by navigating according to your values.

**E–Excel in relationships.** Loyal relationships flow from God's love. *Credibility* is revealed through humility, trust, competence, and clarity. When we put others first, depend on Him, soar with our strengths, and know our values, credibility is produced. Build credibility by excelling in relationships. Credibility develops loyal relationships by positively answering the question: "Can I trust you?"

## Endnote

1. Charles Swindoll, *Growing Strong in the Seasons of Life* (Portland, OR: Multnomah Press, 1983), 58.

# Chapter 19

# Shine with Perseverance

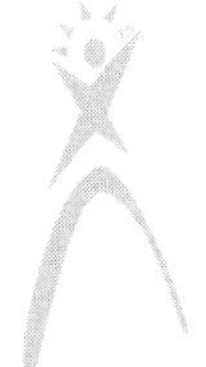

## CAN I COUNT ON YOU?

*Consider it pure joy my brothers whenever you face trials of many kinds, because you know that the testing of your faith develops perseverance. Perseverance must finish its work so that you may be mature and complete, not lacking anything*
(James 1:2-4).

After many years of dependable service to his boss, an elderly carpenter sat down in the contractor's office to break the news that they both knew was inevitable. "As much as I have loved my job, boss, I can't go on," the old man said. "My bones ache, and I need a rest. Please accept my resignation."

"What will you do next? How will you support yourself?"

"We'll get by. We don't have much money, but we don't have many years either. My wife and I need some leisure time together enjoying our kids and grandkids."

"Well, I am sad to see you go, but I understand. Still, may I ask one more thing of you?"

"Anything you want, boss."

"I want you stay with me to build one more house."

The elderly carpenter wasn't expecting such a large request, but what could he do? He agreed to complete one last job, but he went home grumbling to his wife. "I have already done so much. I can't believe he wants more from me."

The builder did not come to inspect the old man's work during the entire process, and the employee was glad. His heart was clearly not in his work—he just wanted to get the job done—and he resorted to shoddy workmanship, using whatever material was readily available, no matter how inferior. When the carpenter finished his work, the builder finally came to inspect the house. The boss made no comment about the workmanship. Instead, he asked, "Is there anything else we should do to this house before we call the job done? Do you think we should include built-in bookshelves or replace the pine doors with cherry? Is there anything else you recommend we get done before we give the keys to the owner?"

The carpenter looked around and saw many things he could do to make the place a fine home, but he was tired and burned out. "I think its fine, boss," he simply said.

"Very well," said the builder. He handed the front-door key to the carpenter. "This is your house," he said, "my gift to you."[1]

So it is with us. We let our guard down for a second and let up. We build our lives in a distracted way—reacting rather than acting, willing to put up with less than our best. At important points, we decide to coast and not give our full effort. Then, with shock, we look at the situation that we have created and find that we are now living in the house that we have built. If we had only realized, we would have done it differently.

## PRESS ON

God is preparing us for something great, something beyond what we could ever hope for or imagine. Crowns, mansions, and heavenly treasures await those who place their trust in Him. By His grace, our future is set. But let us not forgo today. Too many believers are so focused on tomorrow that they miss the opportunity to represent His Kingdom right here and now. With such a bright future ahead, how can we possibly let "shoddy workmanship" define any of our works today? Our work is a means to represent the Kingdom of God. Let us not ever forget our responsibility to shine everyday in the works that we do as we represent Him both now and forever. In *A Life God Rewards,* Bruce Wilkinson says that there is a direct connection between what we do on earth and what God will do for us in Heaven:

> Simple decisions, such as how you spend your time and money, will become opportunities of great promise. And you will begin to live with an unshakable certainty that everything you do today matters forever.[2]

---

**We are called to press on.**

---

Never forget: When we accept Christ as Lord, we immediately become a part of His Kingdom. It is not just a future Kingdom, but one that is very present and very real—right where we are. His Kingdom is present and thriving today in our families, in our workplaces, and in the world around us. The things we do now to represent the eternal King are preparing us for the rewards and eternal blessings of our everlasting future. We are called to persevere and to press on as God advances His Kingdom through us for all eternity.

## STAND FIRM IN TRIALS

Everything that we hear and imagine about Heaven and God's eternal Kingdom seems so perfect. In contrast, our daily lives can be filled with so many challenges and difficulties. Around each corner of our journeys lie countless problems, trials, and setbacks. Our life at work is no different. Choosing to seek a work life that shines does not mean that everything will be easy. Trials will come our way at work in spite of our commitment to His Kingdom and even because of our commitment to shine. We can count on that.

We often will stumble and make mistakes. I would hate to admit how often I have been discouraged as my company and I have fallen short of our vision to shine with excellence. Some days, it appears that we do the exact opposite of what our vision calls for. Other days, it seems like problem after problem is stacking up against us. We often fail to adequately represent our vision. Yet, we are called to persevere.

We cannot avoid trials, failures, and problems; however, we can choose our response to them. We can decide to be consumed by problems. We can cut and run from them. We can shut down and be defeated by our failures. On the other hand, we can choose to trust God to mature us, complete us, and direct us to persevere and overcome the trials that we face. We can rise up and move on, not defeated by our failures but inspired to grow from them. Learning to endure and overcome is an undeniable requirement of God's plan for those who represent His Kingdom.

> *We can rejoice, too, when we run into problems and trials, for we know that they help us develop endurance. And endurance develops strength of character, and character strengthens our confident hope of salvation* (Romans 5:3-4 NLT).

When we rejoice in our salvation, our problems have a tendency to look much smaller. Great perseverance is found in knowing that God always fulfills His promises. When we trust Him, He uses trials to strengthen our resolve, our character, and our relationship with Him.

## NEVER GIVE UP

A great story of perseverance—of never giving up—comes from one of our top sales representatives. He had been trying for months to get the president of a power company to look at one of our new pieces of equipment. The problem was that this particular customer had experienced problems with one of our machines many years prior and had no intention of considering us for this upcoming purchase. Our representative had diligently pursued this opportunity with phone calls, personal visits, apologies, pleadings, and whatever else he could muster, all to no avail. The customer simply refused to even look at our equipment.

Upon hearing that the company had given an order to our competition for a new piece of equipment, our sales representative decided to try one more thing. He got up really early, picked up a new machine, and parked it in the president's reserved parking space. *"I have nothing to lose in forcing him to look at it,"* he reasoned. It was through this confident act of perseverance that our sales representative received his audience with the president. And, yes, the story has a happy ending. The customer cancelled his order with the competitor and purchased the machine from us. The reason? This customer realized that he could count on our employee to persevere, regardless of the challenge, and to be there for him.

## FIGHT THE GOOD FIGHT

Perseverance is steady, continuous belief and action despite ongoing difficulty or setbacks. Those who persevere are consistent and trustworthy in their actions. They do not turn and run when things get tough. Rather, they resolve to endure through challenging situations. Are you facing any trials in your life right now? List your biggest challenges here:

- ______________________________
- ______________________________
- ______________________________
- ______________________________

Instead of asking *why*, try asking *what*. As it relates to these trials instead of belaboring *why me*, ask God, "What do you want to teach me through this trial?" As you face adversity, consider what God might want you to learn as He uses these difficulties to strengthen your character.

People who persevere through difficulty earn recommendations for their diligence and reliability. True friendships grow in times of trial. We all must face our own trials. God, however, can use these trials to grow our relationships with others and with Him. It is in these times of struggle that we learn and grow the most. Perseverance allows us to continue moving toward God's promise. His promise provides hope and a future. It inspires us to give our best, regardless of how we feel and regardless of the situations around us.

Scripture encourages us to make every effort to press on and to keep the faith. God's promise provides believers with a favorable eternal outcome for each of our life stories. What truly matters in the big picture is our relationship with Him. For those who remain faithful to that relationship and finish strong, the prize for perseverance awaits.

> *I have fought a good fight, I have finished the race, and I have remained faithful. And now the prize awaits me—the crown of righteousness, which the Lord, the righteous Judge, will give me on the day of his return. And the prize is not just for me but for all who eagerly look forward to his appearing* (2 Timothy 4:7-8 NLT).

## SHINE REVEALS PERSEVERANCE

Perseverance is a greatly admired characteristic that captivates people's attention. We all love to hear stories of continued perseverance that culminate with great reward in the end. Through Christ, our own perseverance will lead to a life story concluding with great reward. When Christ shines in us, perseverance is a result.

**S–Serve others**. A heart of servanthood glorifies God by helping others. *Generosity* is exceeding expectations. By going the extra mile, serving the Lord heartily, and working with great enthusiasm we develop the momentum we need to keep moving ahead towards God's promise. Momentum is not easily stopped. When our momentum is strong, trials and temptations are easily overcome. Develop perseverance by serving others.

**H–Honor God.** A soul of faithfulness obeys God's purpose. *Stewardship* is serving Him. By yielding to Him, placing our priority on Him, and taking the perspective that it is all His anyhow, we become empowered by Him. When God works in us, we can rely on His strength to persevere through all life's challenges. Develop perseverance by honoring God.

**I–Improve continually.** A mind of excellence pursues God's vision. *Courage* is taking action. By facing our fears, looking ahead, and taking action we overcome the roadblocks that mark our path. Courage motivates us to keep getting better, to never give up, and to finish strong. Develop perseverance by improving continually.

**N–Navigate by values.** The strength of Integrity rises on godly values. *Confidence* is found in trusting our values. Values lay a foundation, set the standard, and provide the sense of security we need to do good works. Confidence inspires us to fight the good fight, finish the race, and run to win. Develop perseverance while navigating by values.

**E–Excel in relationships.** Loyal relationships flow from God's love. *Perseverance* is revealed through generosity, stewardship, courage, and confidence. When we exceed expectations, serve Him, take action, and trust our values, perseverance is produced. We earn recommendations when others know we will be there through thick and thin. Build perseverance by excelling in relationships. Perseverance develops loyal relationships by answering the question: "Can I count on you?"

---

## Endnotes

1. Source unknown.
2. Bruce Wilkinson, *A Life God Rewards* (Sisters, OR: Multnomah Publishers, 2002), 16.

# Chapter 20

# Shine with Love

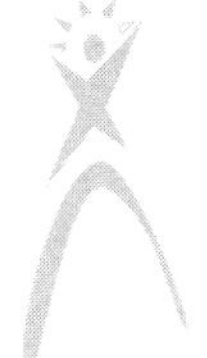

## DO YOU CARE ABOUT ME?

*If I gave everything I have to the poor and even sacrificed my body, I could boast about it; but if I didn't love others, I would have gained nothing*
(1 Corinthians 13:3 NLT).

A few years ago, our company purchased the dealership rights for the island of Puerto Rico. I enjoy the challenge and unique opportunities of doing business in Puerto Rico. I regularly try to visit there and meet with our staff. Anner is a Puerto Rican native who works for us as an equipment sales representative. He has an endearing personality and tremendous potential. He is one of those high-energy types—always running 100 miles an hour. On a recent visit, I ventured outside the normal conversation about equipment and career to ask Anner how things were going at home. His face turned solemn as he explained the sad news of his impending divorce.

At one point in the conversation, I asked him a tough question. "Anner, is your heart right with God?"

While looking at the ground, he answered very quietly, "No, boss. No, it is not. My heart is very dark right now. Every day as I drive home from work, I drive past three churches, but I never go in. My heart feels very dark right now. I know I should go to church. But I don't know which one to go to."

Putting my hand on his shoulder and looking squarely into his eyes, I shared, "Anner, it's not all about going to church. The only way to get your heart right is through the love of Jesus."

His head stooped as he looked back at the ground.

I continued, "Let Jesus into your heart, and He will direct you which church building to go into."

Lifting his head, Anner looked up at me and said, "Boss, don't look at me like that. You make me cry. Please don't look at me like that."

And that's where our brief conversation ended that day.

On the drive back to the hotel where I was staying, I told our Caribbean general manager how I had blown my opportunity to witness to Anner. I asked him to pray for Anner and to pray that someone else would do a better job of witnessing to him than I had. About three weeks later, I received this message from Anner:

> I just want you to know that finally I know what it feels like to be with God. I went into church on Sunday, and my body started to sweat. It did not stop for nearly two hours till finally I found what I need. Others have been telling me that, and I'm sorry for not listening sooner. Now I know what that look you gave me is. That is the look of having peace in your heart. Other Christians have that same look. Now I have that look too. Thank you, Kris, for giving me that look.

The look to which Anner referred has nothing to do with me because I am not capable of giving any other human being a look that could make such an impact. Only the Holy Spirit can do that. I, like many of us, got hung up on trying to say the right things to help "lead someone to Christ." In this case, I felt that my words had obviously fallen short. The real reason I just stood there looking at him was that I did not know what else to say or do! God, however, did not choose to work through my words or works that day. Instead, He chose to open Anner's eyes to see the love of Jesus Christ shining in me. My job at that point was basically to just shut up and shine. I am beginning to better understand that when

I am weak, God is strong. It is not by words or deeds, but by His love, through His power, and in His timing that we are saved.

## LOVE GOD

God is at work all around us, building His Kingdom while reconciling a lost world. We can recommend Christ to others, but only God can build His Kingdom. One of the most effective ways that God grows His Kingdom is through our relationships. The SHINE vision is all about building loyal relationships. It is not about proselytizing or trying to force our beliefs on someone else. It is not found in self-righteous living or in trying to look good. SHINE is not a checklist, a blue print, or a guide to holy living. The SHINE principles simply are based on a loving relationship with Christ that allows God to work in us for His glory. We shine when God works in us to build eternal relationships that glorify Him.

---

**We shine when Gods works in us.**

---

Love is the greatest of all gifts. The apostle Paul wrote, "Three things will last forever—faith, hope, and love—and the greatest of these is love" (1 Cor. 13:13 NLT). No emotion or attitude is stronger than love. Love lasts forever. It is the most important quality that we can exemplify. It is the key to our relationship with God. "Love the Lord your God with all your heart and with all your soul and with all your mind and with all your strength" (Mark 12:30). We owe God our love. He desires it. He demands it. He deserves it. He provides it. And when we return love to the Lover of our soul, we find ourselves filled with more of His love.

## LOVE YOURSELF

Love is the key to all of our relationships. Jesus said, "Love your neighbor as yourself . . . " (Mark 12:31). We often grasp the call to love our neighbors. Harder to fully grasp is Jesus' command for us to love ourselves. We do not have to look far to find people who apparently do not have much love for themselves. At the same time, there are many whose great self-love comes across as self-centered, prideful, and arrogant. The love of self that Jesus refers to is not romantic love, ego love, selfish love, or surface love. He is talking about the type of love that only God provides. He is talking about the love of God that abides in us. " . . . God is love. Whoever lives in love lives in God, and God in him" (1 John 4:16). If we love God, and He lives in us, how could we not appropriately love ourselves? True love for self is found in understanding that we are children of God. When we love and respect ourselves as children of God, we can then love and respect others as children of God, as well.

> *Dear friends, since God so loved us, we also ought to love one another. No one has ever seen God; but if we love one another, God lives in us and His love is made complete in us* (1 John 4:11-12).

## LOVE OTHERS

So what does all of this love of others and self have to do with business? I am not suggesting that you ask your fellow employees to join hands Monday morning and sing *Kumbaya*. I am also not suggesting that you give every customer who walks through your door a big hug accompanied with tears of joy. (Although it might be kind of fun to see their reactions!) No, I am only suggesting that you love God with all that you have. Love Him like you have never loved before. Love Him at work like you love Him at church. Love Him in such a way that others will see your love for Him and His love will shine in you:

> *Those who are wise will shine as bright as the sky, and those who lead many to righteousness will shine like the stars forever* (Daniel 12:3 NLT).

This kind of love for God will fulfill you like you've never been fulfilled before. It will open your heart to loving not only yourself but also others. It will even push you to begin caring for those who may outwardly appear to be unlovable. The sheer radiance of this love will draw others to you for developing new relationships and building enduring trust. These relationships will enable you to shine beyond significance as His love connects others to Jesus Christ through you. The greatest recommendation of all comes in the power of a love capable of forming loyal relationships that last forever. It's true that none of us can live a perfect life, but in Him we can all experience His perfect love.

## SHINE REVEALS LOVE

Nothing attracts the attention of others like God's love. We show our love for God by showing His love to others. Love is how an invisible God becomes visible. The great commandment is all about love. We shine when God's love is seen in us.

> *'And you shall love the Lord your God with all your heart, with all your soul, with all your mind, and with all your strength.' This is the first commandment. And the second, like it, is this: 'You shall love your neighbor as yourself . . . '* (Mark 12:30-31 NKJV).

**S–Serve others.** A heart of servanthood glorifies God by helping others. "You shall love the Lord your God with all your heart . . . " (Mark 12:30). *Humility, compassion, and generosity* lead to an attitude of love. God has called each of us to a mission of service. When we sacrifice our own desires in order to serve others, we reveal the heart of Christ. We shine when God's love is seen in us. "For even the Son of Man came not to be served but to serve others, and to give His life as a ransom for many" (Matt. 20:28 NLT).

**H–Honor God.** A soul of faithfulness obeys God's purpose. "You shall love the Lord your God with all your . . . soul . . . " (Mark 12:30). *Trust, gratitude, and stewardship* lead to an attitude of love. God has a purpose for our work. He has given our work to us as a gift. When God works through us to accomplish His purposes, we reveal the soul of

Christ. We shine when God's love is seen in us. "But seek first his kingdom and his righteousness, and all these things will be given to you as well" (Matt. 6:33).

**I–Improve continually.** A mind of excellence pursues God's vision. "You shall love the Lord your God with all your . . . mind . . . " (Mark 12:30). *Competence, courage, and passion* lead to an attitude of love. God has a vision for each of us. He has gifted us and prepared us to seek His vision. Pursuing God's vision of excellence reveals the mind of Christ. We shine when God's love is seen in us. "You can enter God's Kingdom only through the narrow gate. The highway to hell is broad, and its gate is wide for the many who choose that way. But the gateway to life is very narrow, and the road is difficult, and only a few ever find it" (Matt. 7:13-14 NLT).

**N–Navigate by values.** The strength of integrity rises on godly values. "You shall love the Lord your God with all your . . . strength" (Mark 12:30). *Clarity, conviction, and confidence* lead to an attitude of love. God desires that we develop Christ-like character. Our lives are a process of character development that prepares us for eternity. Godly values reveal the strength of integrity found in Christ. We shine when God's love is seen in us: "Therefore everyone who hears these words of mine and puts them into practice is like a wise man who built his house on the rock. The rain came down, the streams rose, and the winds blew and beat against that house; yet it did not fall, because it had its foundation on the rock" (Matt. 7:24-25).

**E–Excel in relationships.** Loyal relationships flow from God's love. "You shall love your neighbor as yourself" (Mark 12:31). Life is all about *love.* God is love, and He lives in those who love Him. His love is the source of all of our relationships. We shine when God's love is seen in us. "A new command I give you: Love one another. As I have loved you, so you must love one another. By this all men will know that you are My disciples, if you love one another" (John 13:34-35).

*Credibility, perseverance, and love* answer the question: "Do you care about me?"

Conclusion

# Beyond Significance

Business acquisitions are often painstaking. Such was the case when our company recently purchased another dealership in a nearby state. It took five years to seal the deal. We got close several times, but for a number of reasons, we could not close the transaction. Confident that God was leading us to move forward in this acquisition, our company kept pursuing this opportunity to acquire this new statewide territory. One of the times that we were close to sealing the deal, we felt that God was telling us to move forward and hire an outstanding former employee named Scott to run this potential operation. Although this guy had no desire to leave where he was currently working, he was open to what God might be orchestrating in his returning to work for our company. Scott told me, "Where I am, I can accomplish all of my personal and professional goals, but I feel if I return to your company I will be able to impact people for eternity. I want my work to make a difference for eternity."

With a proven leader on board, we again moved forward with the acquisition and set a closing date for the purchase. As we drew up the final paperwork, Hurricane Ivan tore through this new territory. For a company that sells tree equipment, a storm presents a substantial opportunity for increased sales. Understandably, the owner again took the deal off of the table in order to benefit from this potential upswing in business. Now we had a key employee who had left a great job to join our company for a position that now might never exist. We started questioning whether God really was leading us toward this acquisition. Most of us felt led to persevere. A few suggested that we just give up on the whole thing. Time went by, and again the opportunity presented itself. This time, we were able to close the deal and expand our company.

As soon as we finalized the deal, we could tell that God had indeed called us to make this acquisition. When I met with and shared the SHINE vision with our new employees, most of them heartily embraced it. Many mentioned that they had never seen a company so bold about their faith. Most were very positive about being a part of our company, except for one employee: the prior owner's son-in-law, Mickey. While he was cordial, it was obvious that he was not buying into what we were saying. Time progressed, and things went well with the transition. Sales revenues proved much higher than expected. We were thrilled with the new employees that we had retained. We were even able to add some other key members to the team. We had projected a small financial loss, at best, in the first year of operation. However, we were pleasantly surprised to turn a respectable profit, which definitely exceeded our expectations.

Normally revenue, employee retention, and profitability would have been the most valuable rewards of a successful acquisition. In this acquisition, however, we gained something more. Loyal relationships developed in the transition process. Together, we all grew and improved, as well as strengthened our vision to shine with excellence. At his annual review, I asked Scott what was he the most proud of in his first year of running the new business. His answer took me by surprise. He smiled and said, "Mickey." He then proceeded to explain in more detail.

It turned out that Mickey had always envisioned that he would be one of the owners of the dealership. Our purchase had taken away this dream. When we came in with our new plans and shared our SHINE vision, he was skeptical and really did not want any part of it. However, he stayed with the company. Mickey's expertise in a certain line of our equipment allowed him to travel around to our various locations and help out. Over time, as he visited our stores, he began to see that the SHINE vision was more than just words. Wherever he would visit our locations, our people were good to him. They treated him with respect and made him feel like a valuable member of the team. One day, while working with one of our sales representatives, Mickey shared some struggles that he was dealing with. Our sales rep asked if he could pray for him. Mickey was shocked that someone would want to pray for him while they were at work.

A few days later, Mickey accepted Jesus Christ as his Savior. Mickey told Scott, "Now I know why you guys got to buy this business instead of me. I would have never been saved in a church, or anywhere else, for that matter. The only place I could come to Christ is at work. You guys showed me how cool it is to be a Christian, even at work. Because of that, I have found Jesus." A few weeks later, another employee told Mickey about some personal struggles. And Mickey recommended Jesus Christ as the answer!

The SHINE vision continually manifests itself through stories such as this—many of which I never hear. But that's exactly how God works. We don't always know when it is happening. However, when God works in us, He makes eternal differences for His Kingdom. When Christ shines in us, His impact reaches beyond significance. Over time, I have come to realize there are four stages that we pass through in our careers. We continually must choose which of these stages or levels we will perform at. I call these stages the four levels of performance:

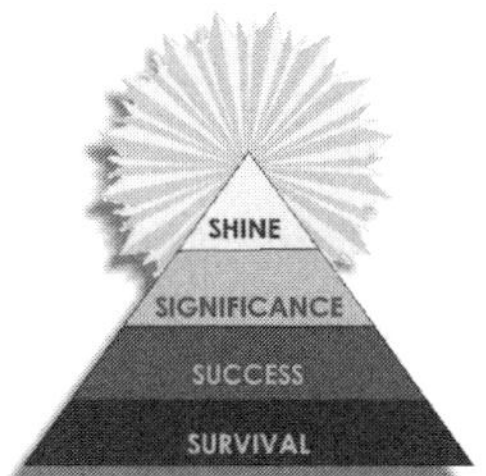


## Level 1: The Survival Level

Level 1, the Survival Level, is when the sole justification for our work is to meet our own personal needs. On this level, work is just a means to a paycheck and a way to get by. When we operate on the Survival Level, our work has very little meaning. Motivation is low. At the Survival Level, we are motivated only by earning a buck. We work so that we can survive. Many workers spend their entire careers on the Survival Level, begrudgingly serving their time at work. They only do enough to get by. On the Survival Level, workers usually perform to a minimal standard for their position. Therefore, work performance is low on this level. Workers frequently complain about their work, typically think they deserve better, and usually blame others for the situation that they are in. Rarely is there personal gratification or fulfillment on this level. *Survival is what we do to get by.*

### Level 2: The Success Level

One step beyond the Survival Level is Level 2: the Success Level. When we operate on this level, motivation is high. We see something that we want, and we do whatever it takes to get it. The Success Level tends to be all about us. More possessions and higher status drive us to work harder. Personal achievement becomes the goal of success. The Success Level produces workers with high external motivation. They crave more money, power, and victories. High performance is common on this level. An attitude of "winning is everything" is widespread at this level. Competition runs high on the Success Level. Some of the highest-achieving employees work on this level. Performing well on the Success Level can result in personal gratification. However, there is little to no true fulfillment. The Success Level is all about self-promotion and personal gratification. *Success is what we do for ourselves.*

### Level 3: The Significance Level

The third level, the Significance Level, is very rewarding. Significance reaches way beyond success. Success is something that we do for ourselves; significance positively affects the lives of others. The impact of significance spreads and multiplies. The greater the good we do for others, the higher the significance of our work climbs. Helping others becomes the goal of significance. The Significance Level produces workers with high internal motivation. Instead of focusing on individual achievement, they focus on helping others reach their goals. An attitude of serving others is common at this level. Teamwork runs high on the Significance Level. Performing well on the Significance Level brings fulfillment in our work. Personal gratification on this level comes by helping others find success. The Significance Level is all about promoting others and making an impact through them. *Significance is what we do for others.*

### Level 4: The SHINE Level

The final level is the level beyond significance. It is the highest level that we can ever attain. We cannot reach it alone. When we shine, we do not have to worry about survival: It is already accomplished. When we shine, success is a given. When we shine, we significantly impact the lives of others. As a light encompasses the darkness, the Shine Level encompasses all the other levels of performance. Shine is not something that we can do on our own. *Shine is when God works in and through us.*

## LET GOD'S LIGHT SHINE

Unfortunately, many of us spend way too much time on the lower levels of this pyramid. On the Shine Level, where true fulfillment is found, Christ shines in us. He shines in us as we seek:

- God's mission of service.
- God's purpose of faithfulness.
- God's vision of excellence.
- God's values of integrity.
- God's relationships of love.

When our focus is on God, and we depend fully on His light, the future will always be bright.

Still, there are times that we don't shine at all. The worries and desires of this life constantly beckon from the darkness. In the darkness, we chase our own dreams and make selfish decisions for our own benefit. Without a clear focus on following Christ, the challenges of life take their toll. Anger, frustration, guilt, shame, pride, and all the other powers of the darkness conspire to bring us down. By relying on our own power, our faith decreases, weakness increases, and our sins take firm hold. The darkness so quickly can engulf us. Yet, in the midst of darkness there is always hope.

> *I am the light of the world. If you follow Me, you won't have to walk in darkness, because you will have the light that leads to life* (John 8:12 NLT).

The key to overcoming the darkness is found in simply letting go of our own will and desires by trusting His light to illuminate the way. The more we rely on Him, the more transparent we become and the brighter He will shine in and through us. For in our own transparency, we can no longer rely on ourselves but on the Light of the world shining in us. Inspired by His vision and consumed by His presence, we rise from the darkness. And by the power of His light, we reflect His glory.

- With a heart of servanthood, we serve others.
- With a soul of faithfulness, we honor God.
- With a mind of excellence, we improve continually.
- With the strength of integrity, we navigate by values.
- When we love others as we love ourselves, we excel in relationships with others and, most importantly, with God.

> *You are the light of the world—like a city on a hilltop that cannot be hidden. No one lights a lamp and then puts it under a basket. Instead, a lamp is placed on a stand, where it gives light to everyone in the house* (Matthew 5: 14-15 NLT).

God provides the light we need. He empowers us to shine right where we are for His glory. In Him, our lives can have purpose and make an eternal difference for His Kingdom. He sets the choice before us. We must choose survival, success, significance, or SHINE.

For those of us who choose to shine, our work is no longer just what we do for a living. Rather, it is an ordained calling, a way of living—of standing out like a lamp atop a hill—where God ignites our lives to shine beyond significance.

> *Let your light so shine before men, that they may see your good works and glorify your Father in Heaven* (Matthew 5:16 NKJV).

## ABOUT THE AUTHOR

**Kris Den Besten** currently serves as president/CEO of five national and international companies which have experienced a cumulative growth in annual sales of $6 million to $100 million while under his leadership. Beyond his corporate responsibilities, Kris is a board member of a ministry for the under- and unemployed which teaches God's principles for work and then places graduates with jobs that provide hope and a future.

As a seminar and conference speaker, Kris teaches that each of us are called to real life ministry and that Kingdom-focused business is a key tool God is using to carry out the Great Commission. With early training as a television sportscaster, Kris is a down-to-earth, from-the-heart communicator who effectively connects with pastors and business leaders, church members and business professionals, both male and female when speaking at corporate events, churches, and through media.

Kris is a founding partner of Real Life Resources, Inc., a not-for-profit ministry focused on transforming life and work. For more information about SHINE conferences and workshops for a church or business group, visit: www.shinevision.com.

Contact Kris Den Besten at kris@shinevision.com or through:
Real Life Resources
4401 Vineland Road, Suite A-15
Orlando, FL 32811
www.realliferesources.com

Additional copies of this book and other book titles from DESTINY IMAGE are available at your local bookstore.

Call toll-free: 1-800-722-6774.

Send a request for a catalog to:

**Destiny Image® Publishers, Inc.**
P.O. Box 310
Shippensburg, PA 17257-0310

*"Speaking to the Purposes of God for This Generation and for the Generations to Come."*

**For a complete list of our titles, visit us at www.destinyimage.com**